TEQUILA
MOCKINGBIRD

TEQUILA MOCKINGBIRD

COCKTAILS with a LITERARY TWIST

10th Anniversary Expanded Edition

TIM FEDERLE

ILLUSTRATED BY
LAUREN MORTIMER

RUNNING PRESS
PHILADELPHIA

Copyright © 2023, 2013 by Tim Federle
Interior and cover illustrations copyright © 2023, 2013 by Lauren Mortimer
Cover copyright © 2023 by Hachette Book Group, Inc.

Running Press
Hachette Book Group
1290 Avenue of the Americas, New York, NY 10104
www.runningpress.com
@Running_Press

Printed in China

Originally published in hardcover and ebook by Running Press in April 2013.
First Revised Edition: March 2023

Published by Running Press, an imprint of Perseus Books, LLC, a subsidiary of Hachette Book Group, Inc. The Running Press name and logo are trademarks of the Hachette Book Group.

The Hachette Speakers Bureau provides a wide range of authors for speaking events. To find out more, go to www.hachettespeakersbureau.com or call (866) 376-6591.

The publisher is not responsible for websites (or their content) that are not owned by the publisher.

Print book cover and interior design by Josh McDonnell.

Library of Congress Control Number: 2022021966

ISBNs: 978-0-7624-8263-4 (hardcover), 978-0-7624-8274-0 (ebook)

RRD-S

10 9 8 7 6 5 4 3 2 1

For Brenda Bowen—
worth her weight in Cuervo Gold

CONTENTS

Part 1

Part 2

Part 3

Part 6

A Loaf of Bread and Thou:

Bonus!

INTRODUCTION

....

Gentle Drinker:

Nearly ten years ago, I shot off an email to my literary agent: "Wouldn't it be funny to create a literary cocktail book featuring punny recipes that riff on classic books?" She agreed, and on a whim, I threw together a proposal that caught the eye of a young editor at Running Press. She bought the book, I popped Champagne, and then . . . I had to figure out how to write it.

All these years later, a project created on a lark became one of the all-time bestselling cocktail recipe guides, spawning sequels and spinoffs, and—imitation *is* the sincerest form of flattery—dare I say, copycats.

Big anniversaries deserve big rethinks, and in this very special updated edition, I've partnered with famed cocktail-recipe creator Cody Goldstein to improve the recipes and take them to the next level. We've also added a handful of brand-new drinks inspired by modern books that have emerged in the last decade, and we've carefully reorganized everything into contemporary categories.

From barflies to book clubs, welcome to *Tequila Mockingbird: Cocktails with a Literary Twist*. Go ahead and pull up a stool. Or a recliner, for that matter.

Don't worry if you snoozed your way through Comp Lit. Think of this recipe guide as SparkNotes with a liquor license, trading out pop quizzes for popped corks. For all you mixologists and cosmo-connoisseurs out there, we're serving up your favorite recipes with a smart new twist. You've gotta have something to talk about behind the bar—why not raise the level of banter by brushing up on your Brontë?

There are beverages here to suit all tastes. We begin with In Vino Veritas, classic recipes with classy twists. From **A Rum of One's Own** to **Crime and Punish-mint** to **Drankenstein**, we've got Freshman English covered. In Roll Out the Barrel: Bevvies for Book Clubs, we've concocted some stirring brews, which will goad even the quietest book club attendees to voice an opinion. **Hazy Rich Asians**, **The**

Hand-Mule's Tale, **Little Fireballs Everywhere**—the hits don't stop!

With Just Add a Parasol: Summer Reading, we give you the best protection from the sun—the shade cast by a book open above your face, and a handy-dandy, hydrating beverage by your side. From **The Joy of Sex on the Beach**, to **Fahrenheit 151**, to **How the Garcia Girls Lost Their Aperol Spritz**, you're bound to stay far too long at the beach with these hotties on deck. And you'll finally understand what Bradbury meant when he wrote, "It was a pleasure to burn."

Then we switch gears with Read 'Em and Weep: Beautiful Books to Make You Ugly-Cry, because what's a reader's life without a radical shift in tone? You're bound to shed a Hollywood tear from **Call Me by Your Nectarine**, to **Tequila Mockingbird**, to the **Interpreter of Midoris**, so get camera-ready.

And fret not, non-drinking readers! We've got nonalcoholic drinks for you, too, that recall gentler, less wobbly times. No shame in sitting back while the freshmen make fools of themselves.

If your buzz is on but your belly's empty, we've cooked up **The Deviled Egg Wears Prada**, **I Know This Munch Is True**, **The Mustard Yellow House**, and a handful of other bar bites for book hounds. Should you find yourself surrounded by a group of hesitant readers—or card-carrying library-goers—try our drinking games. You'll be reading your friends under the table . . . you know, if they're brave enough to take a shot every time Dickens introduces a new character.

Relax. We won't get too stuffy. After all, the only things needed to enjoy a good book are a lamp and a place to sit. An effective cocktail should be just as easy. For those who don't know their Bloody Mary from their Mary Shelley, flip the page for a quick refresher on the tools, techniques, and terms used throughout this book. Trust us: If you've got a Solo cup and a corner store, you can make 90 percent of these recipes 100 percent of the time.

So grab a glass, already. Let's get a little stupid and look a little smart. Even if you don't have a BA in English, tonight you're gonna drink like you do.

TOOLS

....

GLASSWARE

COCKTAIL (OR MARTINI) GLASS (4 TO 6 OUNCES): Drinks are shaken and strained into this long-stemmed, iconic V-shaped beauty.

COLLINS GLASS (10 TO 14 OUNCES): Built like a highball glass, but taller and narrower. Best for icy, very large, tropical drinks.

FLUTE (4 TO 6 OUNCES): Champagne cocktails are served in this specially designed stemware, which showcases the bubbles without letting too many of them fly free.

HIGHBALL GLASS (10 TO 12 OUNCES): Midway between a rocks and a Collins glass, but taller than the former and shorter and fatter than the latter. If you could only have one book on a desert island, you'd choose wisely; if you could only have one glass, you'd choose this.

MASON JAR (1 CUP TO ½ GALLON): Though generally used for bottling preserves, this also makes a great container for down-home, country drinks.

MUG (10 TO 12 OUNCES): The hardworking coffee cup does double duty for hot alcoholic drinks.

PINT GLASS (16 TO 20 OUNCES): An all-purpose beer-chugger, this glass tapers at the bottom, and some have a "bulb" near the lip to give the brew a better head.

ROCKS (OR LOWBALL OR OLD-FASHIONED) GLASS (6 TO 10 OUNCES): A drink poured "on the rocks"—that's over ice, rookie—is frequently served in one of these short, heavy tumblers.

SHOT GLASS (¾ TO 2 OUNCES): For ~~slamming back~~ calmly enjoying a variety of aptly named "shots." The smallest of drinking vessels, these are also handy as measuring devices.

SOLO CUP (16 OUNCES): A plastic red cup that is a typical dorm room and party staple. In a pinch, used for basically every drink ever.

EQUIPMENT

BLENDER: For frosty, feel-good frozen beverages. Make sure yours can handle ice like a champ.

JIGGER: For small liquid measurements. A metal hourglass shape, available in a variety of sizes. We prefer the 1-ounce-over-1½-ounce model—but you should up the dosage if you're trying to get through *Anna Karenina*. And just drink straight from the bottle if you're attempting *Walden*.

JUICER: The classy crowd prefers their lemons and limes (and pomegranates, thank you very much) freshly juiced, whether by hand or by machine—but we won't balk if you go the bottled route. On average, lemons and limes produce about an ounce of juice each.

MEASURING CUPS AND SPOONS: Duh, right? Dry cups typically range from ¼ cup to 1 cup. For larger liquid measurements, it's easiest to have a standard 2-cup glass measuring cup. Measuring spoons go from ¼ teaspoon to 1 tablespoon.

MUDDLER: Grown-up term for fruit masher. Releases oils and flavors in mints and berries.

PITCHER AND PUNCH BOWL: Best for serving all the nonfiction characters in your life. Half-gallon pitchers always do the trick; same with a gallon punch bowl.

SHAKER: An essential device that need not intimidate! Our fave is the *Cobbler*: a three-part metal contraption (counting the capped lid) with the strainer built right in. The other varieties are the *Boston* (a glass mixing cup and metal container) and the *French* (basically a *Cobbler* shaker sans strainer). Both require a separate strainer, and that's valuable time you could be reading—or drinking.

STRAINER: Like a sifter for liquids. If you ignored our advice to buy the all-in-one *Cobbler* shaker, you'll want to pick up a *Hawthorne* strainer, which will fit tight into your shaker's metal mouth. The *Hawthorne* filters only the liquids (not the ice) into a cocktail.

VEGETABLE PEELER (OR CHANNEL KNIFE): A handy shortcut for creating twists (see: Garnishes, page 8), the peeler removes a thin layer of skin from fruit to add flavor and color.

TECHNIQUES

MAKING A DRINK

FILLING: In some recipes, you're asked to "fill" your glass to the top with a final ingredient—typically Champagne, club soda, or cream. The amount of liquid needed depends on how large your glass is: from 2 to 4 ounces for a flute, to anywhere from 4 to 8 ounces for rocks, highball, or Collins glasses.

FLOATING: To create pretty layers in the drink, "float" one liquid on top of the other. The easiest method is to invert a spoon and slowly pour liquor/liqueur over the back of the head, letting the liquid pool without breaking the cocktail's surface—sort of like trying not to cry while reading *A Thousand Splendid Suns*.

ICING PUNCHES: For parties, blocks of ice are a cinch. Simply fill a clean, empty milk carton with water, freeze overnight, and peel away the waxy paper.

MUDDLING: In some recipes, once you've filled a glass with the specified fruits, juices, or herbs, use a *muddler* (page 6) to gently mash the ingredients, twisting lightly to release oils and flavors.

RIMMING: Rub the lip of the desired glass with a lemon or lime wedge, then "rim" the glass (hey, now!) by turning it upside down and placing the rim on a plate of salt, cocoa powder, sugar, or whatever the recipe calls for. Then gently rotate the glass so the rim gets coated in the desired ingredient.

SHAKING: Fill a *Cobbler* tin with all of the ingredients and ice, cap shut, and shake vigorously—harder than you think, bordering on "workout." Uncap the lid and strain into a glass.

STIRRING: Experts use a barspoon, which has a long, twisting handle, but an everyday cereal spoon will do just fine. For cocktails with carbonation, the bubbles do the stirring for you.

DECORATING A DRINK

GARNISHES: Like a truly memorable book cover (remember the puppeteer's hand on *The Godfather*?), garnishes are the promise of something special to come. Technically, *garnish* adds both color and flavor (like a lime wedge or a lemon twist), *garbage* is any food or fruit that's solely for aesthetic purposes (like a lemon wheel), and *kitsch* is something hokey (like an umbrella, or the entire plot of *Valley of the Dolls*).

Garnish techniques include:

TEARING: The easiest way to include mint in a cocktail. Simply wash, remove stems, and take out your frustration one rip at a time.

TWISTS: Delicately flavor a drink and add a little citrus pizzazz. The official method involves a *channel knife*, which peels a long, thin gouge out of a lemon. Our easier, preferred method is to wash a lemon and then use a *vegetable peeler* to remove a 2-inch strip of skin. Fold in half, twist over drink, wipe the rim of the glass with the twist, and then drop into the glass.

WEDGES: The most widely seen lemon or lime garnish. Wash, dry, and cut the ends off the whole fruit. Then chop the fruit in half "the short way" and quarter the remaining halves. Wedges can either be squeezed and dropped into the drink, or balanced on the rim after cutting a notch into the fruit.

WHEELS: Circular disks of fruits or vegetables. Wash, dry, and cut the ends off the whole fruit, then slice crosswise into "wheels." Can be placed in the drink, or balanced on the rim after cutting a notch into the fruit.

TERMS

SPIRITS

GIN: Distilled from grain and, though flavored with everything from juniper to cinnamon, smells a bit like rubbing alcohol—but in a fun way. Favored by F. Scott Fitzgerald.

RUM: Ernest Hemingway's main hooch is the best sugar-water money can buy. The lightest kinds are the youngest; the darkest may be older than seven years.

TEQUILA: Comes from the blue agave plant, not the cactus. The word "tequila" itself refers to a very specific region in Mexico, and the authentic stuff doesn't harbor any wayward worms. Kerouac adored it.

VODKA: Odorless and clear, vodka is typically distilled from potatoes and grains. Russians drink it straight, but Americans mix it up—William S. Burroughs in particular.

WHISKEY: Distilled from grains and hailing from the US, Canada, Ireland, or Scotland. Dorothy Parker's prized drink is serious stuff by its lonesome, but it plays nice with others. We feature both rye whiskey and bourbon, which is any good Southerner's definition of whiskey.

LIQUEURS

Strong, syrupy spirits that are flavored any number of ways, from fruits to flowers; also includes schnapps. The following liqueurs make appearances throughout: *absinthe* and *ouzo* (licorice-like flavor); *amaretto* (almond/apricot flavor); *anise* (brands like Galliano and Herbsaint); *blackberry, butterscotch, cinnamon* (a brand like Goldschläger); *cherry* (a brand like Heering); *coffee* (a brand like Kahlúa); *crème de cassis* (blackcurrant flavor); *crème de menthe* (mint flavor); *elderflower* (a brand like St-Germain); *hazelnut* (a brand like Frangelico); *limoncello* (lemon flavor); *melon, orange* (generics like triple sec and Curaçao; a brand like Grand Marnier); *peach schnapps*, and *sour apple schnapps*.

BEER

A malt brew and a hoppy flavor. Recipes in this book focus on lagers, specifically light beer and—good luck here—malt liquor.

WINE

Fermented juice from myriad fruits and grapes. In subcategories, we feature: *brandy*, generally a distillation of wine or fruit juice; *sweet vermouth*, a fortified wine, flavored with herbs; *sherry*, a brightly sweet, fortified wine hailing from Spain; and *Champagne*, a sparkling white wine from a specific French region.

OTHER FLAVORINGS

AGAVE NECTAR: A widely available sweetener, it goes down like honey with an exotic accent.

BITTERS: The cologne of cocktails, added in small amounts to give a drink depth and nuance. *Angostura* and *Peychaud's* are the two aromatic bitters featured in this book. The latter is a slightly sweeter, fruitier version of the former, and both are strong and majestic. We also use *orange bitters*, any brand of which will showcase a bright citrus flavor.

COARSE AND SEA SALT: The rough, grainy seasoning favored by foodies.

COCONUT CREAM: A bottled, sweetened coconut product (a brand like Coco Reál Cream of Coconut) for tropical drinks.

GINGER JUICE: Made from the liquid content of ginger root, ginger juice is not just a blast of flavor, it's also a digestive aid.

GRENADINE: A sweet red syrup that's a snap to make, and loads better than the corporate, high-fructose junk sold to bars.

GRENADINE SYRUP

Boil 2 cups bottled pomegranate juice (a brand like POM Wonderful) with 2 cups granulated sugar in a medium saucepan. Stir for 5 minutes—until it's reduced to half the original volume—into a syrup. Bottle and keep in the fridge for up to three months. Or days, if you party like us.

HOT SAUCE: Available in any number of brands, all featuring a peppery kick.

ORGEAT: A sweet syrup made from almonds, sugar, and orange.

PALM SYRUP: A sweet syrup made from palm sugar. Note that simple syrup made from brown sugar can be used as a substitute.

WASABI PASTE: A Japanese condiment—you've seen it next to sushi— that goes down hotter than *Lady Chatterley's Lover.*

WORCESTERSHIRE SAUCE: Contains everything from anchovies to molasses, and adds a steak-sauce slurp to certain cocktails.

IN VINO VERITAS
THE CLASSICS

> I like to have a martini,
> Two at the very most.
> After three I'm under the table.
> After four I'm under the host.
> —Dorothy Parker

What do number two pencils, Converse high-tops, and *Pride and Prejudice* have in common? They're one hundred percent, bona-fide classics. Every book in this section is a literary standard and can be found in almost any library or thirty-four-year-old storage unit. Each of these old-style titles deserve a primo spot on your bookcase or digital library, and you deserve some delicious drinks to down while savoring the taste of stories that have stood the test of time.

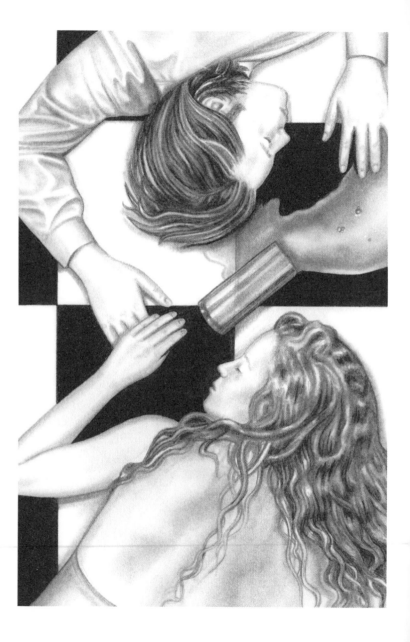

ROMEO AND JULEP

ROMEO AND JULIET (CIRCA 1597)
WILLIAM SHAKESPEARE

With the play's original title sounding like Shakespearean surfer slang—*The Most Excellent and Lamentable Tragedy of Romeo and Juliet*—this melancholy romance is for anyone who has fallen in love with the hot boy from the other side of the tracks. Who *can't* relate to the star-crossed lovers, doomed from the start by parents who, like, just don't understand? With a tragic, poisonous finale, this historic work created the mold, inspiring not only adaptations (*West Side Story* is just *R and J* with jazz hands), but also an entire road map for young-love stories. Fall under the spell of a drink so spring-like and peach-fuzzy, you might be forgiven for not realizing its full effects.

- **6 sprigs fresh mint**
- **½ ounce brown sugar syrup**
- **½ cup peaches, sliced**
- **1½ ounces bourbon**
- **1 (12-ounce can) seltzer**
- **3 dashes Angostura bitters**

In a highball glass, muddle the mint, brown sugar syrup, and peaches until the sugar dissolves like a relationship over summer break. Add ice and bourbon, and fill to the top with the seltzer. Stir in the bitters. Prepare to fall in love—fast.

ORANGE JULIUS CAESAR

JULIUS CAESAR (CIRCA 1599)
WILLIAM SHAKESPEARE

Friends, Romans, upperclassmen: With pals like this, who needs enemies? Shakespeare's *Julius Caesar* reads like a luxuriantly extended definition of the word "backstabber," as the title character's rise to power inspires those closest to him to plot his assassination. Though Caesar gets top billing, he actually appears in only a handful of scenes; the real star here is Marcus Brutus, proving that sometimes a secondary player can walk away with the show. Sneak a little mother's milk into an old-fashioned breakfast recipe—and trust us (no, really, you can trust us), the result is pretty killer.

3 ounces orange juice
3 ounces prosecco
1½ ounces light rum
1 ounce heavy cream
1 ounce simple syrup
¼ teaspoon vanilla extract

Have your closest frenemy load all the ingredients, plus a handful of ice, into your blender. Only *after* he removes his fingers, get whir-ring. Serve in a Collins glass.

PARADISE SAUCED

PARADISE LOST (1667)

JOHN MILTON

An apple a day may keep the dentist away, but the Devil's no doctor. *Paradise Lost,* Milton's seventeenth-century blank verse poem (don't hold your breath for Dr. Seuss rhymes here), was one of the first examples of Christian literature to paint Adam, Eve, and even your old friend Satan in gray strokes—it's less good versus evil than complicated versus conflicted. Remarkably, Milton didn't just *write* a twelve-part book, he *spoke* it: The author was blind, so he had to dictate the entire text to some kind of angel. Toast Milton's godlike effort with a recipe that features a sinful apple at its core. It'll be worth the price tomorrow morning.

Sugar, for cocktail rim (page 7)
2 ounces apple cider
1½ ounces vodka
½ ounce apple brandy
½ ounce pure maple syrup
¾ ounce fresh lemon juice

Rim a chilled cocktail glass in sugar and set aside. Shake the rest of the ingredients with ice and strain into the glass. No need to justify your ways to anyone once you've had a glass or two of this heavenly liquid.

GULP-IVER'S TRAVELS

GULLIVER'S TRAVELS (1726)
JONATHAN SWIFT

Our grandparents knew *Gulliver's Travels* as a blistering satire wrapped in droll travelogue: An Englishman lost at sea stumbles upon a handful of bizarre lands in which he is by turns the biggest and the smallest creature for miles, leading him to question everything from patriotism to religion to his very definition of home. *You* know *Gulliver's Travels* as the critically panned, audience-ignored film that featured Jack Black putting out a fire by peeing on it (hope you took off the 3-D glasses for that part). In our beachy keen nod to the hero washed ashore, choose your own adventure with a Lilliputian shooter or Brobdingnagian cocktail. Try saying *that* three times drunk.

2 ounces coconut water
1 ounce pineapple juice
½ ounce vodka
½ ounce grenadine syrup (page 11)

Shake the ingredients with ice and strain into an empty rocks glass; this goes down in a single swig. For the bigger, Brobdingnagian variation on the above, double all ingredients, shake with ice, and strain into a cocktail glass. Little seasick? Eyes on the horizon, sailor.

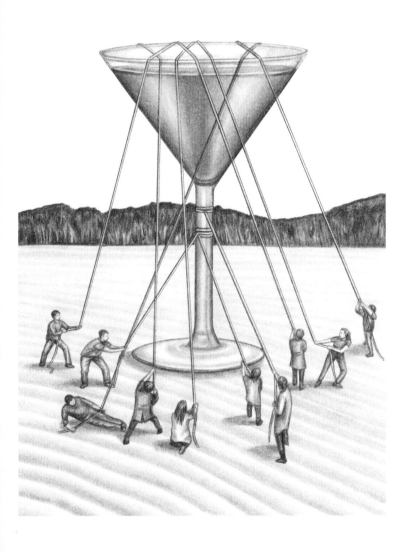

RYE AND PREJUDICE

PRIDE AND PREJUDICE (1813)
JANE AUSTEN

Austen's frothy nineteenth-century masterpiece, which brought the author little acclaim during her short lifetime follows a family's efforts to marry off its five daughters, one of whom leads the narrative. Unfortunately, Elizabeth—famously played onscreen by Keira Knightley's cheekbones—has a judgy streak that practically overshadows the love she has for Mr. Darcy, a stuck-up (but rich!) gentleman. Not to worry: There's a delectable wedding (or four) in the end. We match-make two strong personalities—spicy rye and zingy grapefruit—for an unexpected marriage that'll get folks drinking, dancing, and dropping old judgments.

3 ounces grapefruit juice
1½ ounces rye whiskey

Pour the ingredients over ice in a rocks glass, stirring like a nervous heart. We hold no prejudice against marrying up, but you sure as heck don't need a castle (or a king) to be queen.

DRANKENSTEIN

FRANKENSTEIN (1818)
MARY SHELLEY

Mary Shelley created more than a monster when she anonymously published *Frankenstein* at age twenty-one—she also birthed one of pop culture's greatest misattributions: Frankenstein is the name of the obsessive mad scientist, *not* the green-faced, peg-necked creature. (He gets his own nicknames, including "vile insect" and "wretched devil," courtesy of his dear old dad.) Experiment with the following Halloween-ready, bright green concoction. Heads-up: More than a few couples have played their own version of doctor after downing more than a few of these.

1 ounce tequila
1 ounce green apple juice
1 ounce melon liqueur
½ ounce fresh lemon juice
½ ounce honey
1 (12-ounce) can club soda
2 green grapes, for garnish

Add the tequila, apple juice, melon liqueur, lemon juice, and honey to a shaker with ice. Shake for 5 seconds, then strain into a Collins glass with fresh ice. Top with club soda and skewer grapes for garnish. Now, light a few candles, lock the door, and guard your potion with monosyllabic grunts.

THE S(IDE)CARLET LETTER

THE SCARLET LETTER (1850)
NATHANIEL HAWTHORNE

B elieve it or not, kiddos, there was a time when having a child before marriage wouldn't get you a reality show, but, instead, a very public haranguing. In Hawthorne's *Scarlet Letter*—named after the "A for adultery" badge of dishonor the leading lady has to wear—Puritan New England serves as the case study of a world at odds with religion, hypocrisy, and desire. We push a drink purist's envelope by popping a few cherries (hey, now!) into a sweet and sour standby. This sidecar's so tasty, you might end up parading through town afterward, just like the heroine herself. Have no shame: This baby's all yours.

Sugar, for cocktail rim (page 7)
1½ ounces Cognac
1 ounce blood orange juice
½ ounce cherry liqueur (we like Heering)
½ ounce orange Curaçao

Rim a chilled cocktail glass in sugar and place aside. Shake the rest of the ingredients with ice and strain into the glass. You'll give this one a grade A.

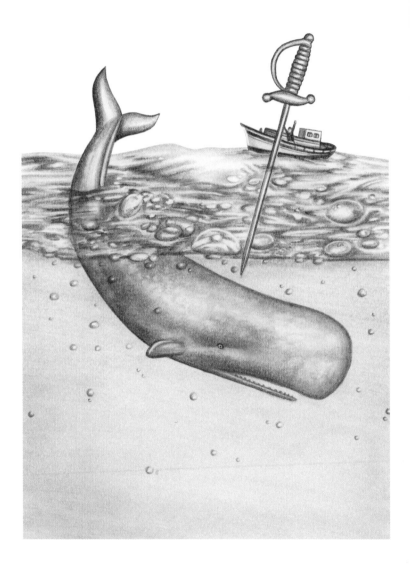

MOBY-DRINK

MOBY-DICK (1851)

HERMAN MELVILLE

This one'll make you think twice about flushing a goldfish down your toilet. In Melville's *Moby-Dick*, published first in England (and greeted with scathing reviews!), the titular whale is best known for attacking Captain Ahab's ship and then—talk about special skills—chewing off the poor fella's leg. Ahab spends the rest of his career limping around, determined to exact revenge on Moby-D, only to finally spear the whale and—Plan B!—get dragged underwater to his own ironic death. Our sea-inspired cocktail is as blue as the Pacific, but the real fun is in playing fish hunter. Grab a harpoon and get even.

1½ **ounces light rum**
½ **ounce grapefruit juice**
½ **ounce fresh lime juice**
½ **ounce blue Curaçao**
1 **(12-ounce) can ginger beer soda**
1 **Swedish Fish candy, for garnish**

Combine the rum, grapefruit, lime juice, and blue Curaçao over ice in a highball glass and fill to the top with the ginger beer. Now for the demonic part: Grab that Swedish Fish by the gills, spear it with a swizzle stick, and get plunging. Just don't fall in yourself.

THE **TURN** OF THE **SCREWDRIVER**

THE TURN OF THE SCREW (1898)
HENRY JAMES

In a rolling country estate—the kind that always wins set designers their fifth Oscar—things are getting spooky for the new governess. In prolific author Henry James's novella, ghosts are after the new hire's charges, and she's determined to keep the tykes safe. Trouble is, nobody else seems to *see* these tricky apparitions, and more than a century after publication, even literary scholars are still scratching their heads: Was the governess a fabulist, or was this a real haunted house? A true classic holds up to different interpretations, and we offer two ways into the Screwdriver—giving you twice the opportunity to check for ghosts in the bar.

Theory 1: She's perfectly levelheaded.
4 ounces orange juice
2 ounces vodka

Theory 2: She's truly haunted.
4 ounces sparkling orange soda (like Orangina)
2 ounces vanilla vodka

For either variation, pour the ingredients over ice in a highball glass. If drinking alone, this may be better enjoyed in a plastic tumbler— just in case someone (or something) sneaks up behind you.

CRIME AND PUNISH-MINT

CRIME AND PUNISHMENT (1866)
FYODOR DOSTOYEVSKY

When the lead character compares himself *favorably* to Napoleon, you turn off the laugh track on page one. New readers of *Crime and Punishment*—the tortured tale of a man who feels destined to murder a pawnbroker and then redistribute the wealth—might think they're tuning in for a literary *Law & Order*. Those readers would be wrong. Crime? Sure! But punishment? Forget primetime courtroom scenes, because the only punishment here is the murderer's life sentence of guilt. Pair vodka with just enough caffeine to give you the shakes. The mint should calm your nerves before you do anything *too* crazy.

1½ ounces vodka
½ ounce coffee liqueur
½ ounce crème de menthe liqueur
1 ounce brewed espresso
½ ounce simple syrup

Add the vodka, liqueurs, espresso, and syrup to a shaker with ice and shake. Strain over fresh ice in a rocks glass. Repeat as needed. Hey, you only live once.

GIN EYRE

JANE EYRE (1847)

CHARLOTTE BRONTË

You know what's too tragic to be funny? A feminist survivor story published under a male pseudonym. With Charlotte Brontë writing as Currer Bell, *Jane Eyre* (think: Gloria Steinem in a bonnet) is the retrospective of an abused orphan-child turned bored teacher-girl turned lovesick governess-lady. Unfortunately, her groom already has a wife—Brontë didn't give the heroine any breaks—and Jane sets off on a soul-quest, refusing subsequent marriage proposals and eventually landing the man, a kid, and the (burned out) home. Brontë wasn't so lucky; she died while pregnant, less than ten years after *Jane* debuted to acclaim. Raise a glass of English gin to a legendary lady, worthy of a sweeter finish than befell her.

> **2 ounces English gin**
> **1 ounce fresh lemon juice**
> **1 ounce honey**
> **8 sprigs fresh mint**
> **3 dashes orange bitters**

Add the ingredients to a shaker with ice, with bonus points if you tear the mint leaves first. Shake well and strain into a cocktail glass. Now nurse that drink like a good nanny.

HOWARDS BLEND

HOWARDS END (1910)

E. M. FORSTER

Sad that the writer of "Only connect"—*Howards End*'s epigraph—had such a tortured time doing so himself. Edward Morgan (E. M.) Forster, the long-closeted novelist of the literary masterpieces *A Room with a View* and *A Passage to India* (the last book he'd write for fifty years, until his death), imagined three distinct families in *Howards End*, an English estate at the center of class tensions, inheritance resentments, and the rare death-by-falling-bookcase. Here, we blend the three distinct flavors of the vintage "Janet Howard" cocktail, for a posh but pronto drink. This'll have you connecting in no time—with other people, God willing, not toppled furniture.

2 ounces brandy
½ ounce orgeat syrup
2 dashes Angostura bitters

A perfect drink for the day you receive word your wealthiest relative has finally ~~kicked the bucket~~ passed on. Shake the ingredients with ice and strain into a cocktail glass—and gather the bravery to ask if you were left anything in the will.

ETHAN POM

ETHAN FROME (1911)
EDITH WHARTON

Talk about a tough winter: Edith Wharton packed this one full of snowstorms, adultery, and—anyone for sledding?—a full-on suicide mission, headfirst into a tree. We reckon that if tragic hero Ethan, tragic zero Zeena, and merry mistress Mattie had been alive during the self-help era, they could've worked out that love triangle in an old-fashioned, nationally televised quarrel. But don't call us prudes—if they'd had a lick (or two) of our snowscape-inspired *Ethan Pom* slushy, who knows? They might have giggled their way into literature's first thruple.

1 ounce Champagne
2 ounces pomegranate juice
3 ounces grenadine syrup (page 11)

Pour the Champagne and pomegranate juice into a rocks glass and then pack with shaved or crushed ice. Drizzle the syrup on top. Now, go for a stroll through town with your most cherished partner-in-crime. (Just don't let your real significant other find out.)

THE PITCHER OF
DORIAN GREY GOOSE

THE PICTURE OF DORIAN GRAY (1890)
OSCAR WILDE

B oy, did this book have it all: knife fights, magic paintings, and (spoiler alert!) people who never age. Wilde wasn't just ahead of the cosmetic surgery boom here—he also pushed the envelope on homoeroticism, resulting in widespread censorship in later versions of the book. Try getting your hands on the juicy early copies of *Dorian*, and then gather a group of aging beauty queens (or simply aging queens), who'll be guaranteed to love our hedonistic youth serum. Just keep them away from your expensive art.

MAKES ABOUT 8 DRINKS
10 sprigs fresh mint
3½ cups iced Earl Grey tea
½ ounce ginger juice
1 cup honey
2 cups vodka (like Grey Goose)
Cucumber, sliced into wheels, for garnish

Tear the mint, then place in the pitcher. Add the Earl Grey tea, ginger juice, and honey. Pour in the vodka and stir. Serve over ice, garnish with the cucumber wheels, and remember: Age before beauty—if anyone will fess up.

THE COUNT OF MONTE CRISTAL

THE COUNT OF MONTE CRISTO (1844–45)

ALEXANDRE DUMAS

Alexandre Dumas knew a thing or two about keeping an audience tuned in. Heck, he knew a thing or *eighteen*, because that's how many newspaper installments it took to tell *The Count of Monte Cristo*, which still sets the bar for archetypical revenge tales. You know the protagonist's formula: (1) Get wrongfully convicted; (2) Go to jail; (3) Get out and get even. Oh yeah, and (4) Get *rich* along the way—the kind of rich that can fill a Jacuzzi with Champagne. Turn the bubbles up high and hop into our sweet-as-vengeance Cristal cocktail. Be warned: It could take prison-worthy deeds to snag the really pricey stuff.

¾ ounce Cognac (like Grand Marnier)
Champagne (like Cristal), to fill

Pour the Cognac into your fanciest flute and top with the best bubbly you can buy. (And if you *can* afford Cristal? Lose the liqueur, double the good stuff, and—hold up—can you Venmo me fifty bucks?)

THE **YELLOW WALLBANGER**

"THE YELLOW WALLPAPER" (1892)
CHARLOTTE PERKINS GILMAN

Not recommended for our readers dwelling in studio apartments: Gilman's classic feminist short story traces one woman's Gothic descent into madness, locked in a bedroom by her physician husband who can't acknowledge that her stultifying marriage may have made her a tad depressed. The hubby's plan backfires when the wife grows more and more desperate, becoming convinced that her makeshift prison cell's yellow wallpaper has somehow trapped other women within. We'd tear down the wallpaper for a recipe that's lasted the ages: bright as a yellow sun and sure to get you out of bed.

1½ ounces vodka
½ ounce amaretto
4 ounces orange juice
½ ounce Galliano liqueur

Combine the vodka, amaretto, and orange juice over ice in a high-ball glass. Give it a stir. Pour the Galliano on top, letting it stay just barely afloat—sort of like your sanity after one (or more) of these.

TWENTY THOUSAND LEAGUES
UNDER THE SEA BREEZE

TWENTY THOUSAND LEAGUES UNDER THE SEA (1870)
JULES VERNE

Translated, adapted, sometimes even copied (see: *Finding Nemo*, among others), this dazzling adventure by Jules Verne, the French father of science fiction, was shockingly prescient in its depiction of future underwater technologies. A time-tested tale of "Boy meets fish, fish turns out to be secret submarine, submarine never lets boy leave because *now he knows too much*," *Twenty Thousand Leagues* sends readers into chilly ocean depths, where they meet eccentric scientists, memorable sea monsters, and one very unforgiving whirlpool. Swirl up your grandfather's Sea Breeze recipe with a little carbonation—and settle old scores by serving this one with calamari.

  1½ ounces vodka
  1 ounce grapefruit juice
  3 ounces cranberry juice
  1 (12-ounce) can club soda

Combine the vodka and juices over ice in a highball glass, and fill to the top with the club soda. Drink slowly to avoid the bends—and come up for air every now and then.

ONE HUNDRED BEERS
of SOLITUDE

ONE HUNDRED YEARS OF SOLITUDE (1967)
GABRIEL GARCÍA MÁRQUEZ

The most celebrated work by Latin America's prince of prose, *One Hundred Years of Solitude* traces one family's multigenerational triumphs and devastations in establishing a South American settlement. Pressing hard on the symbolism pedal, Márquez uses the colors yellow and gold like a weaver, threading death and wealth throughout a story of inevitable decline. We borrow his palette, pairing South America's most famous beer—Cusqueña, the "gold of Incas"—with a cheery, yellow lemonade. The result is so lightweight, you can water your solitude down with a hundred of these—give or take your dignity.

2 ounces fresh lemon juice
2 ounces simple syrup
6 ounces light beer (like Cusqueña)
1 or 2 dashes Angostura bitters
Pinch of sea salt

Pour the lemon juice and simple syrup into a chilled pint glass. Fill to the top with beer and add a dash or two of bitters, along with the salt. Now, sit back and prepare for life's ups and downs . . . you know, with another drink standing by.

DECLINE AND FALL DOWN

DECLINE AND FALL (1928)

EVELYN WAUGH

Don't worry, we're not gonna get all moralist on your ass (you're thinking of *The History of the Decline and Fall of the Roman Empire*, six volumes through which you dutifully napped). No, this is the breezily English satire *Decline and Fall*, Evelyn Waugh's delicious take on university life. Meet Paul Pennyfeather: Booted out of Oxford for streaking through campus (like you haven't done worse), Pennyfeather ends up as the head of a boys' school in Wales, where he becomes engaged to a wealthy sugar mommy—whose cash secretly comes from the South American brothel industry. Get lost in your own Peruvian bordello with help from pisco, a South American grape brandy that pairs fast and fun with standard cola.

1 ounce pisco

1 (12-ounce) can cola

Pour the pisco over ice in a highball glass and fill to the top with the cola. These go down so quick, you could end up half naked on the quad.

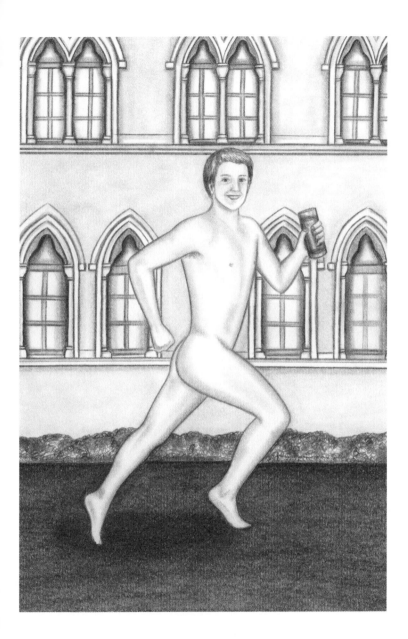

A RUM OF ONE'S OWN

A ROOM OF ONE'S OWN (1929)
VIRGINIA WOOLF

Oh, Virginia. So smart. So sad. So . . . specific. According to our gray Woolf, a woman needs "money and a room of her own if she is to write fiction." (She says nothing of *non*fiction, so apparently you can be broke and living with three other girls in a studio apartment if you're going the journalistic route.) We couldn't agree more with Ginny's recipe for storytelling success, though we'd add another thing to the list: a nice warm cocktail. Prepare the following bevvy on a writerly, wintery night. Who needs a partner around with a drink this hot?

½ cup salted butter, at room temperature
1 teaspoon light brown sugar
¼ teaspoon ground cinnamon
¼ teaspoon cloves
¼ teaspoon nutmeg
Pinch of sea salt
2 ounces dark rum
Cinnamon stick, to garnish

Place the butter, sugar, and spices into a bowl and mix well with a metal spoon. Add batter into a mug, then pour in the rum and fill to the top with hot water, then stir. Garnish with a cinnamon stick. And now? A long walk on the beach, preferably to the lighthouse.

BRAVE NEW SWIRLED

BRAVE NEW WORLD (1932)
ALDOUS HUXLEY

Imagine a world dominated by antidepressants and governmental control over reproductive rights. (Oh. Wait.) Written in the thirties, *Brave New World* could've been copy-and-pasted from today's headlines. Huxley penned a dystopian world in which embryos are preprogrammed for certain behaviors and needs, and technology is so revered that "Oh my Ford" is a commonplace utterance. While Huxley was an outspoken fan of psychedelic drugs, you can *legally* freeze your own brain with a swirly smoothie featuring a surprising aphrodisiac: watermelon. Hey, what you drink (and who you drink it with) ain't nobody's business but your own.

1 ounce vodka
1 cup seedless watermelon, chopped into coarse cubes
¼ ounce fresh lemon juice
½ ounce simple syrup
½ ounce elderflower liqueur

Add the vodka, watermelon, lemon juice, simple syrup, and a handful of ice to a blender, running until smooth. Pour into a cocktail glass and float the liqueur on top. No matter what your political leanings, one gulp of this and you'll be more than brave enough to fight The Man.

LORD PIMM

LORD JIM (1899)

JOSEPH CONRAD

Jim is a young seaman who fancies himself a hero—only to abandon a ship full of Mecca-bound pilgrims when tragedy literally strikes. (Note: If you wanna make some serious coin, go back a hundred years and write about conflicted men at sea.) Told out of chronological order in an innovative, multi-narrator format, *Lord Jim* can nonetheless get a tad stuffy. Spice these Brits up with a famous English beverage that'll turn any host into a hero.

    **1 cucumber, sliced thin into wheels, including 1 wedge
       for garnish
    2 ounces Pimm's No. 1
    1 (12-ounce) can lemon-lime soda
    Lemon wedge, for garnish**

Place several cucumber wheels in a Collins glass, fill with ice, and pour in the Pimm's. Fill to the top with lemon-lime soda, squeeze and drop a lemon wedge into the glass, and garnish with a cucumber for serious cred. And for the love of Triton: Serve childlike adults first.

SILAS MARNIER

SILAS MARNER (1861)
GEORGE ELIOT

Penned under the name "George Eliot," Mary Ann Evans's *Silas Marner* is the tale of a man wronged by his church—closely mirroring the author's own disenchantment with religion. It's only after Marner loses his gold fortune (only *after* he's forced to leave town facing false accusations of stealing from his congregation's coffers) that he discovers his true idea of wealth: becoming a father. Hailed as a clever critique of organized worship and industrialized England, *Silas Marner* inspires a drink that's a little bitter and a little gold-flecked—sort of like life.

1 ounce Goldschläger
½ ounce Grand Marnier
1 (12-ounce) can ginger ale
3 dashes Angostura bitters

Combine the Goldschläger and Grand Marnier over ice in a highball glass. Fill to the top with the ginger ale and add bitters. Get ready for the next best thing to holy water.

THE **OLD MAN** AND THE **SEAGRAM'S**

THE OLD MAN THE SEA (1952)

ERNEST HEMINGWAY

Pulitzer winner drowning in biblical allegory, *The Old Man and the Sea* was Hemingway's final published work in a career dripping with awards and accolades—and alcohol. The premise is simple (and familiar to readers of *Moby-Dick* and enjoyers of Moby-Drink on page 27): An old man sets out to destroy a fish in an act of single-minded delirium. During an epic three-day battle in which the marlin is finally defeated, hitched to the side of the boat, and—hey, old chum!—eaten by sharks en route to shore, the old man emerges weary but victorious. Do your best sailor imitation with the standby gear of any fisherman: whiskey and bait.

2 ounces whiskey (like Seagram's)
1 (12-ounce) can ginger beer
Brandy-soaked maraschino cherry, to garnish

Warning: You're gonna need a bigger glass. Combine the whiskey and ginger beer over ice in a highball glass. Grab some fishing tackle (looks like a fish; has a hook), give it a soapy scrubbing, and then bait 'n' float your cherry. Or, lose the glass and fill a fisherman's flask. Just don't sip and sail.

THE **MALTED FALCON**

THE MALTESE FALCON (1930)

DASHIELL HAMMETT

Unless you're a senior at P.D.U. (that's Private Detective University), ninety bucks says you skipped *The Maltese Falcon*, a popular pulpy novel that became a gun-for-gun film retelling with Humphrey Bogart as a cynical spy for hire. Though it may read like a series of tropes today, Dashiell Hammett's shady cast of femmes fatales and jewel thieves practically wrote the playbook for crime fiction—and the subsequent film noir boom it helped get off the ground. Speaking of which, our simple swill will have you flying higher than a falcon figurine. Slam with suspicion, 'cause this one goes down as gritty and unsentimental as any good private eye.

8 ounces malt liquor
1½ ounces amaro (we like Cynar)

Pour the malt liquor into a chilled pint glass and the amaro into a shot glass. Drop the entire shot, including the glass, into the malt liquor, and enjoy. Now, watch the door and keep one finger on the meta-phorical trigger. You're staying in for the night after one of these.

ROLL OUT THE BARREL
BEVVIES FOR BOOK CLUBS

> Too much of anything is bad, but too much Champagne is just right.
>
> —Mark Twain

Uh-oh. Your turn to host that well-intentioned book club again? Worried your idea of literature (Nicholas Sparks) might not live up to the group's (*Nicholas Nickleby*)? Relax. Any of the following time-tested classics should inspire both a hot debate and a cool drink. The stories in this section will certainly liven and loosen up any book club. Heck, these drinks might even give you enough liquid courage to finally admit that you can't tell your Oxford comma from your elbow.

ONE FLEW OVER

THE COSMO'S NEST

ONE FLEW OVER THE CUCKOO'S NEST (1962)
KEN KESEY

Kesey's groundbreaking novel, written while he was a student at Stanford, was drawn from his stint as a psych ward employee—when he wasn't volunteering in LSD "trials" on the side. (The late fifties weren't all *Leave It to Beaver*, gang.) Though narrated by a paranoid side-character, the hero of the story is McMurphy (Jack Nicholson in the firecracker film version), who leads his fellow patients in a rebellion against Nurse Ratched, a needle-wielding vixen who represents the tyranny of society—and seriously raises the question "Who's the *real* crazy here?" Liberate your own hemmed-in ways with a Cosmo you'd be cuckoo to pass on.

1½ **ounces vodka**
1 **ounce tart cherry juice**
½ **ounce Grand Marnier**
½ **ounce fresh lime juice**

Combine the ingredients with ice in a shaker. Shake well and strain into a chilled cocktail glass. Code blue: It's hard to stop at just one of these.

BLOODY CARRIE

CARRIE (1974)
STEPHEN KING

Children can be so cruel. Sixteen-year-old Carrie White is already a social outcast when she adds every girl's nightmare to the list: having her first period in a gym class *shower*. It gets messier from there, with scheming teens setting Carrie up to win prom queen, only to crown her not with a tiara, but—can't get *this* at Walmart—with pig's blood. Little do her fellow classmates know about Carrie's secret telekinetic powers (it's a Stephen King novel after all, his first to get published), and our heroine buttons the novel with a fair impression of Satan going through puberty. Spice up a legendary drink with ingredients even a schoolgirl has on hand—though there's no way you're serving this to a sophomore.

5 ounces tomato juice
2 ounces whiskey
½ ounce fresh lemon juice
1 teaspoon grated horseradish
½ teaspoon Worcestershire sauce
¼ teaspoon celery salt
¼ teaspoon sea salt
¼ teaspoon cracked black pepper
10 dashes hot sauce
1 piece well-cooked bacon, to garnish

Add all the ingredients, except the bacon, to a shaker with ice. Shake well and strain over fresh ice in a Collins glass. Traditionalists would finish with a celery stalk, but we like to live high on the hog.

ARE YOU THERE GOD?
IT'S ME, MARGARITA.

ARE YOU THERE GOD? IT'S ME, MARGARET. (1970)
JUDY BLUME

Move over, wizards. Make room, vampires. For many of us, Margaret was the original YA superstar, even if her epic battles were of the religion-and-puberty kind. (Actually, *especially* because of that.) Point is, Margaret showed us how to face all of life's big ol' quandaries, from God to boys to bra size. Ninety bucks says when Maggie got to college, she faced an even headier question: How the hell do you make a margarita without a blender? (Hint: On the rocks, kid.) Don't worry, Madges of the world, we've got your back. We'll even hold your hair when you've had one too many.

> **Coarse salt, for cocktail rim (page 7)**
> **1½ ounces tequila**
> **1 ounce fresh lime juice**
> **½ ounce triple sec**
> **1 lime wedge, for garnish (optional)**

Rim a Solo cup in coarse salt and set aside. Dump all your feelings—er, *ingredients*—into a shaker with ice. Shake well and strain over fresh ice in the salted Solo cup. Or, if you're feeling classy, strain into a cocktail glass and garnish with a lime wedge. This is in Judy Blume's honor, after all.

FRANGELICO AND ZOOEY

FRANNY AND ZOOEY (1961)
J. D. SALINGER

A cat named Bloomberg, a dude named Zooey, and a girl who smokes in the tub: We spy hipsters! Originally appearing in two *New Yorker* installments as part of a larger series about the Glass family, J. D. Salinger's *Franny and Zooey* concerns a college coed who is so at wit's end with campus poseurs and politics, she faints while at a restaurant with her boyfriend. He flees—hell, there's a football game—and Franny's left chanting a prayer, all by her kooky lonesome. With a religious wink to Frangelico, the nutty liqueur in a monk-shaped bottle, find your center by icing down those troubles over some decaf.

2 ounces decaf espresso, chilled
½ ounce hazelnut liqueur (like Frangelico)
½ ounce mezcal
½ ounce simple syrup
1 ounce heavy cream

Put on a cardigan, a jazz album, and a frown. Then pour the espresso, liqueur, mezcal, and syrup over ice in a rocks glass, floating the cream on top. Not smiling yet? For the love of Brooklyn, be thankful you've got this much time—and this little responsibility—to feel so full of angst. It won't last forever, baby!

A CONFEDERACY OF OUNCES

A CONFEDERACY OF DUNCES (1980)
JOHN KENNEDY TOOLE

Originally handwritten on piles of paper, *A Confederacy of Dunces* found life only after its author lost his own; John Kennedy Toole committed suicide, his mother found those secret pages, and she began toting her late son's novel around their home state of Louisiana, claiming it was the next great American novel. (Sorry, guys: Sometimes moms are right.) Now a universally adored Pulitzer-winner, starring an oddball, slightly delusional New Orleans slacker, this classic goes best with another: the Big Easy's own Sazerac. Raise a glass to the tragically shortchanged Toole—and everything else he might have written.

1 teaspoon anise liqueur (like Pernod)
1 ounce rye whiskey
1 ounce Cognac
¼ ounce simple syrup
3 dashes Peychaud's bitters
Lemon twist, for garnish

Pour the liqueur into a chilled rocks glass, swirl around 'til the sides are nice and coated, and then toss anything that doesn't stick. Add the remaining ingredients to a shaker with ice, shake well, and strain into the glass. Guests? Lemon twist garnish. No guests? Cut the cute and get reading.

THE **HAND-MULE'S TALE**

THE HANDMAID'S TALE (1985)
MARGARET ATWOOD

In Atwood's anxiety-attack-inducing novel, a hardcore Christian society has taken over the US government and renamed the country the Republic of Gilead. Highly patriarchal and repressive, Gilead is organized into castes, where women sit at the bottom and are forbidden to read, write, own property, handle money, or have any control over their own reproductive rights (sound familiar?). Our heroine, Offred, belongs to the section of the female populace called Handmaids, whose sole purpose is to bear the fruit of the upper echelon's loins. It all goes downhill from there—you're gonna want a stiff drink after this one.

3 strawberries, cut in half
4 blackberries, cut in half
1 ounce vodka
1 ounce Cognac
½ ounce fresh lime juice
1 (12-ounce can) ginger beer
1 whole strawberry, for garnish
1 whole blackberry, for garnish

Add the sliced strawberries and blackberries to the bottom of a Collins glass. Pour the vodka, Cognac, and lime juice into the glass and add ice. Top with ginger beer and garnish with 1 whole strawberry and 1 whole blackberry. Put on your red cloak and drink it down fast.

BRIDGET JONES'S DAIQUIRI

BRIDGET JONES'S DIARY (1996)
HELEN FIELDING

So what constitutes a classic, anyway? *We* say anything that gets people reading, sharing, and, in the case of *Bridget Jones's Diary*—a British smash turned international vacation read turned swoon-worthy movie—belly laughing. Reading just like your own diary, only with double the cigarettes and half the men (we're being nice), Bridget tells her *Pride and Prejudice*–inspired tale as a thirty-something singleton on the prototypical quest for real love. With a nod to her ongoing list of New Year's resolutions, we go bubbly with a relatively healthy daiquiri that even Bridget would enjoy. Do your duty and have one for her.

½ cup large, fresh strawberries (about 4)
2 ounces Champagne
1½ ounces light rum
½ ounce fresh lime juice
½ cup frozen pineapple chunks

Remove the greens from the strawberries—this is a drink, not a *salad*—and combine them in a blender with Champagne, rum, lime juice, frozen pineapple, and a handful of ice. Blend until smooth and serve in a cocktail glass. And now? Take a sip of courage and let's finally create that online dating profile.

THE JOY LUCK CLUB SODA

THE JOY LUCK CLUB (1989)
AMY TAN

Ah, legacy. Amy Tan's multigenerational Chinese saga—recounted by a veritable family reunion of narrators—is one that anyone with a verbose relative can relate to (I'm talking to you, Grandpa). Nothing gets a story primed like a pair of loose lips. Pull out those old photos and get busy mixing up this variation on a popular Chinese restaurant standby, sweet as a fortune cookie and twice as lucky.

MAKES ABOUT 4 DRINKS
1½ cups light rum
1½ cups orange juice
½ cup club soda
¼ cup grapefruit juice
2 ounces brandy
2 ounces orgeat syrup
4 lychees, for garnish

Add the ingredients, plus two handfuls of ice, to a festive bowl. Grab four straws and get gabbing—perhaps finally asking Pap Pap how Grandma became a world-famous Mahjong champion.

THE RYE IN THE CATCHER

THE CATCHER IN THE RYE (1951)
J. D. SALINGER

The most celebrated work by a legendarily reclusive author, *The Catcher in the Rye* spoke directly to the disenchanted, angsty youth of the fifties—and still echoes vibrantly to first-time novelists who pray their coming-of-age protagonist will be favorably compared to Holden Caulfield. Narrating from a mental ward, Caulfield colorfully recounts his times in and out of prep school, chasing (and getting rebuffed by) sex workers, while gaining bloody noses, enemies, and overnights on train station benches. Throw together a traditional Christmas punch for an untraditional Christmas story: Much of *Catcher* takes place over the holidays, and this one ought to lift the spirits of your crankiest elf.

MAKES ABOUT 8 DRINKS
½ bottle (about 1½ cups) rye whiskey
4 ounces pineapple juice
2 ounces fresh lemon juice
1 liter ginger beer

Add the whiskey and juices to a punch bowl with a big ol' hunk of ice (page 7). Stir in the ginger beer and gather your pals. Time to chase those blues away.

INFINITE ZEST

INFINITE JEST (1996)
DAVID FOSTER WALLACE

Ten Commandments–size cast populates this rule-breaking modern classic, infamous for sprawling prose, endless footnotes,[1] and a madcap depiction of the future.[2] Confounding and delightful in equal measure, *Jest* takes place in the 'burbs of Boston,[3] between a halfway house and a nearby tennis academy. Wallace had one of his central characters take his own life, and in a tragic true-life twist, Wallace did the same, leaving behind a magnum opus that will be argued and digested for infinity. Serve up a tennis-ball-yellow cocktail that mimics the zest and bounce of one fallen literary legend.

1 ounce vodka
1 ounce limoncello
1 ounce Midori liqueur
½ ounce fresh lemon juice
Club soda, to fill

Minding that tennis elbow, shake the ingredients with ice and strain into a cocktail glass. Head back to the court, sport, and never give up on your game.

---

1 Just like this, but they appeared at the end of the book—over four hundred of 'em!

2 Time is marked with corporate sponsorships, as in Year of the Perdue Wonderchicken.

3 Wallace briefly studied philosophy at Harvard (who hasn't?) and later taught at Emerson.

THE **ADVENTURES**

OF **SHERBET HOLMES**

THE ADVENTURES OF SHERLOCK HOLMES (1891–92)
SIR ARTHUR CONAN DOYLE

Pro-tip: "Elementary, my dear Watson" was never *exactly* spoken by
Sherlock Holmes. Conan Doyle's beloved sleuth appeared on the big
screen saying that phrase, but not on the page; he was too busy being the
only detective who could crack a case from the comfort of his armchair.
We take a tip from a lesser-known story that appeared alongside twelve
others in a blazingly popular magazine series: Raise a glass to "The Blue
Carbuncle," a Holmes whodunit involving a goose with a very expensive
gem lodged very inconveniently in its neck. After you trade jewels for
berries, the only remaining mystery will be why you've never made this
party pleaser before.

MAKES ABOUT 10 DRINKS
1 quart berry sherbet
1 bottle (about 3 cups) Champagne, chilled
1 liter ginger ale
½ cup fresh blueberries, for garnish

Empty the sherbet into a punch bowl and pour the Champagne
and ginger ale on top. Float the blueberries and serve. Don't leave
the room for long—you'll return to a fast-empty bowl and a classic
whodrunkit.

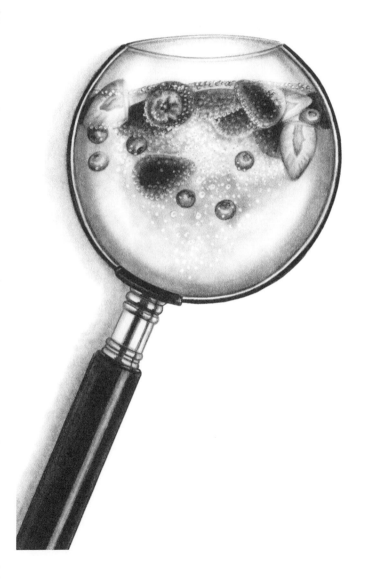

LITTLE FIREBALLS
EVERYWHERE

LITTLE FIRES EVERYWHERE (2018)
CELESTE NG

Where there's smoke there's fire, and there is *plenty* of both in this page-turner from Celeste Ng. Buttoned-down Elena Richardson follows all the rules. That's how she keeps everything under control—husband, kids, house, job. Except, is it really under control? Elena is delighted when *un*buttoned artist Mia Warren and her daughter Pearl move into her rental property. But Pearl and the Richardson kids become a tad too close, and when a racially tinged custody battle splits the town apart, sparks fly between Elena and Mia. And between Elena and her husband. And her kids. And her house—which burns to the ground (on page 1, so no spoiler). Keep a bucket of water nearby as you turn up the heat with these little flaming fireballs.

1 ounce single malt whiskey
1 ounce Fireball
¾ ounce fresh lemon juice
½ ounce jalapeño-infused honey
½ ounce ginger liqueur
1 red-hot candy

Combine the whiskey, Fireball, lemon juice, jalapeño honey, and ginger liqueur in a shaker with ice. Shake well and strain over fresh ice in a rocks glass. Garnish with a red-hot candy. Warning: This one is spicy, spicy, spicy! Lots of smoke and heat, but not enough to burn down the house.

BLACK LEOPARD, RED BULL

BLACK LEOPARD, RED WOLF (2019)
MARLON JAMES

Mermaids and gremlins and witches, oh my! Marlon James's revolutionary *Black Leopard, Red Bull* is so action-packed it makes *Game of Thrones* look like *Goodnight Moon*. Set in a mythical version of ancient Africa, this fantastical novel tells the epic story of Tracker, his band of hunters, and their search for a mysterious lost boy. With revenge and heroism abounding, this head-spinning book defies easy description. Let's just say it features shapeshifters, mages, seekers, villains, heroes, kings, queens, and just about everything in between—not to mention a propulsive narrative style. Read this fully caffeinated or you won't be able to keep up.

1   teaspoon blackberry syrup
1 tablespoon fresh lemon juice
2 ounces orange vodka
½ can of Red Bull
1 lime wedge, for garnish

Pour the blackberry syrup, lemon juice, and orange vodka into a cocktail shaker with ice and shake well. Strain over fresh ice into a tumbler. Add half a can of Red Bull and garnish with the lime wedge. Check for poison before you gulp this down.

HAZY RICH ASIANS

CRAZY RICH ASIANS (2013)
KEVIN KWAN

*C*razy Rich Asians has it all: glamour, glitz, and drama galore, a healthy serving of toxic relationships, classism, terribly fabulous parties, and terribly fabulous secrets—it's *The Great Gatsby* on ecstasy at 3 a.m.! The book's two lovebirds, Nick and Rachel, are from two very different worlds; when Rachel lands in Nick's native Singapore on vacation, only to find out he's more loaded than Mr. Monopoly and Scrooge McDuck combined, all hell breaks loose in the most opulent way imaginable. We've concocted a drink that will fly you (on a private jet) to far-off lands.

1½ ounces Baijiu
1 ounce lychee juice
1 ounce mandarin juice
¼ ounce agave nectar
3 ounces Champagne
Edible gold leaf, to garnish

Combine Baijiu, lychee juice, mandarin juice, and agave in a shaker with ice. Shake well and strain into a Champagne flute. Top with Champagne and garnish with an edible gold leaf. But only if you're engaged to a billionaire—or imagine you should be.

BIG LITTLE LIMES

BIG LITTLE LIES (2014)
LIANE MORIARTY

Who didn't gulp down this book about a tight group of Australian mums with too much time, too much money, and murder on their hands? Or maybe you devoured it when it moved to the small screen (and super-gorgeous Monterey) with #bonus Meryl Streep. If you've never read or seen this perfect crime drama, you're in for a treat: five women, a bunch of kids, a nasty bully, lots of unsavory men, and a killing that can't be pinned on anyone. Or can it? For sheer glamour, intrigue, twisted plot twists, and revenge, *Big Little Lies* can't be beat. Cool off from the steamy shenanigans with this Lime Ziggy, which no one will need to bully you into quaffing down.

2 ounces gin
1 ounce fresh lime juice
½ ounce melon liqueur
¾ ounce simple syrup
1 (12-ounce can) ginger beer
Lime wedge, for garnish

Combine the gin, lime juice, melon liqueur, and simple syrup in a shaker with ice. Shake well and strain over fresh ice in a stemless wine glass. Top with ginger beer and garnish with a big lime. Delicious, and that's the truth.

THE MANHATTAN WE BECAME

THE CITY WE BECAME (2020)
N. K. JEMISIN

Mix two parts fierce geopolitical dystopia with three parts speculative fiction, throw in a giant, ghostly-white, multi-tentacled creature that smacks down the Williamsburg Bridge in the first few pages . . . and you have the modern masterpiece that is N. K. Jemisin's *The City We Became*. Jemisin reimagines the five boroughs of New York City—as embodied by Manny, Brooklyn, Bronca, Aislin, and Padmini—in almost human form, and pits them—kicking and screaming—against a common, terrifying Enemy. Your head may explode as you chart the course of this disunited band of urbanites trying to hold on to the essence of their city—but *whose* city is it? Shake up this extra-strength Manhattan and wait for the end of the world as we know it.

1½ **ounces bourbon**
1½ **ounces rye whiskey**
1 **ounce sweet vermouth**
1 **ounce sherry**
2 **dashes chocolate bitters**
Cherry, large, to garnish

Combine the bourbon, rye whiskey, sweet vermouth, sherry, and bitters into a shaker with two ice cubes. Quickly shake and strain into a rocks glass with one large ice cube. Garnish with a monster cherry and lift a glass to the coming apocalypse.

THE OTHER COGNAC GIRL

THE OTHER BLACK GIRL (2021)
ZAKIYA DALILA HARRIS

Scalp massages, toxic office politics, and dangling modifiers combine in the horror-thriller that is *The Other Black Girl*. Nella, the only Black employee at an old-school publishing company, is doing just fine—other than those iiiitty-bitty micro-aggressions—until Hazel arrives. Hazel is Black, too, and super-friendly, so they have a lot of fun together (Nella finds Hazel's after-work hair-braiding parties especially . . . relaxing). But things get twisty when Nella loses status at work, and scary notes start appearing on her desk. Is Hazel gaslighting her? Is someone else? Or everyone else? By the end of this blockbuster bestseller, Nella is in for a major shock, as are you, dear reader. We suggest soothing your nerves with this smooth concoction.

2 ounces Cognac
1 ounce dry vermouth
3 dashes orange bitters
3 dashes aromatic bitters
1 green olive, for garnish

Add the Cognac, dry vermouth, and bitters into a mixing glass and fill with ice. Stir around 20 rotations and strain into a cocktail glass. Drop in an olive to the bottom of the glass for garnish and don't drink this one at the office alone.

JUST ADD A PARASOL
SUMMER READING

> After all, the best part of a
> holiday is . . . to see all the
> other fellows busy working.
> —Kenneth Grahame,
> *The Wind in the Willows*

Sun's out, buns out, books out, as the saying goes (not necessarily in that order). Honestly, these works of fiction shine so bright that you're going to want to lather a hefty amount of sunscreen on your eyes—perhaps SPF 451. What better way to spend a hot July day than flipping pages and sipping cocktails? So, sit back, shake the sand out of your towel, (apologize to the beach-goer you just shook sand on), and stay hydrated with these summery sips.

A MIDSUMMER NIGHT'S BEAM

A MIDSUMMER NIGHT'S DREAM (1605)
WILLIAM SHAKESPEARE

Take two parts Ren Faire and one part Greek mythology, add a liberal dash of forest-dwelling nymphs, and you've got Shakespeare's whimsical meditation on love and lunacy. An amateur might toast this oft-produced play with two melatonin and a gulp of cough syrup, but Lord, only a foolish mortal would try that—this is a dream, not a blackout. You'll want to stay upright, if drowsily so, for a light, vegetation-heavy drink that will keep you skimming all five acts before a proper fairy-blessed slumber. You might just wake up in love.

8 sprigs fresh mint
4 blackberries
½ ounce fresh lime juice
2 ounces bourbon (like Jim Beam)
1 (12-ounce) can club soda

Muddle the mint, blackberries, and lime juice in a highball glass. Add ice and bourbon, and fill to the top with the club soda. Sip to your imagination's content—stopping only if your shadow begins to speak.

THE LIME OF THE

ANCIENT MARINER

THE RIME OF THE ANCIENT MARINER (1798)
SAMUEL TAYLOR COLERIDGE

Next time you're marooned on an island, resist the temptation to call out, "Water, water everywhere, and not a drop to drink!" First of all, the other survivors don't need a clever quote, they need cocktails and a grief counselor. Second, you'll probably end up dying of dehydration, so your final words ought to be accurate. The *actual* phrase—"Water, water everywhere, nor any drop to drink"—is from an epic poem about bad weather, angry oceans, and pissed-off dead birds who aren't afraid to haunt a hull. (Moral of the story: Leave God's creatures alone, skipper.) Celebrate your land legs with this limey twist on a salty classic—and seriously consider staying back on the beach.

Sea salt, for highball rim (page 7)
2 ounces gin
2 ounces fresh lime juice
1½ ounces grapefruit juice
1½ ounces honey
4 ounces mineral water

Rim a chilled highball glass in sea salt. Fill the glass with ice, pour in the ingredients, and give a good stir. When you're sobered up, matey, head back to the lookout deck—and watch out for low-flying birds.

REMEMBRANCE

OF THINGS PABST

REMEMBRANCE OF THINGS PAST (1913–27)
MARCEL PROUST

If at first you don't succeed, try submitting your 1.5-million-word manuscript again. Such was the fate of Proust's monumental seven-volume novel written over the course of thirteen years(!), (which might as well have been called *Remembrance of Literally Everything Past*), initially rejected by publishers who are now kicking themselves in the grave. A thoughtful exploration on the tricky nature of time-telling, one passage has gained particular fame: Proust's narrator describes how he is suddenly transported back to childhood after tasting a madeleine soaked in tea. Take a journey to simpler times with a delicate summer drink that'll have you recalling your first secret sips of beer. Pair this drink with as many cookies as your memory demands.

3 ounces grapefruit juice
1 (12-ounce) can beer (like Pabst Blue Ribbon)
1 (12-ounce) can lemon-lime soda
Pinch of sea salt
1 grapefruit slice, for garnish

Pour the grapefruit juice and beer into a pint glass and fill to the top with the lemon-lime soda. Add in a pinch of sea salt and garnish with a grapefruit slice. Now, kick back on a hammock, toss back a few madeleines, and pull out those old journals—or start a new one.

LOVE IN THE TIME OF KAHLÚA

LOVE IN THE TIME OF CHOLERA (1985)
GABRIEL GARCÍA MÁRQUEZ

Never settle . . . even for a doctor . . . with a hot accent. Otherwise, you could go a half-century 'til you find the real thing. In Márquez's version of romance, the zipper-straining desire of a trio of lovebirds is practically an illness, eating his characters from the inside out. Here, two teenagers fall in lust, but the girl chooses an MD to settle down with, leaving the boy to choose anything with two legs to settle the score. True adoration knows no calendar, and "fifty-one years, nine months and four days" later (but who's counting?), the two are reunited again after Husband the First dies. Adored as a Colombian treasure, this book deserves a nod that's as sweet as love and as spicy as lust.

1½ ounces aged rum
1 ounce cold-brew coffee
½ ounce coffee liqueur (like Kahlúa)
2 ounces heavy cream
Ground cinnamon or nutmeg, to taste
3 coffee beans, for garnish

Combine the rum, cold brew, and coffee liqueur over ice in a rocks glass. Pour the cream on top and sprinkle a little spice and beans. Now, drink to the heady brew of passion—even if the only foreign doctor in your life is on TV.

FAHRENHEIT 151

FAHRENHEIT 451 (1953)

RAY BRADBURY

It ain't about censorship, kids! Bradbury's then-futuristic *Fahrenheit 451* (the temperature at which a book burns) is about a ~~truly unthinkable~~ society in which technology reigns supreme and books go bye-bye. Written in the fifties but ringing eerily true today, *Fahrenheit*'s world stars firemen who *start* the flames, setting the written word afire and sniffing out pesky, law breaking readers. Serve up a burning-hot party drink to toast the peerless printed page—hey, you don't wanna spill rum on a Kindle. Soon as this one's ready to serve, disconnect the slow cooker (and all your iGadgets) and reconnect with your party.

MAKES ABOUT 10 DRINKS
4 cups apple cider
2 cups orange juice
1 cup cranberry juice
1 cup pineapple juice
6 cloves
4 cinnamon sticks
16 ounces rum (like Bacardi 151)

Pour the ingredients, except the rum, into a slow cooker. Warm for approximately 1 hour, or until heated through. *After* everyone has turned in their cell phones, unplug the pot and add the rum. Give it a stir and ladle away.

THE JOY OF SEX ON THE BEACH

THE JOY OF SEX (1972)
ALEX COMFORT

Keep a legend around long enough and it eventually comes (*ahem*) back into style. Such is the case with *The Joy of Sex*, a cheeky (literally) seventies how-to guide that was modeled after cookbooks, subbing out ears of corn with ears of people. The original pencil drawings—featuring shaggy-haired, "mustachioed" men exchanging coital maneuvers with what appeared to be a grown-up Marcia Brady—have in recent years been expanded upon, fully fleshed out, and updated with all new terms (now introducing: STIs!). Bottom line? This book took the science out of sex and injected it with feel-great fun. Here, we offer our own position on the standby cocktail. Have a ball—and do sip safe.

1½ ounces vodka
1½ ounces orange juice
1½ ounces cranberry juice
½ ounce crème de pêche
1 (12-ounce) can ginger ale

Combine the vodka, orange juice, cranberry juice, and crème de pêche in a shaker with ice. Shake well and strain over fresh ice in a highball glass. Fill to the top with the ginger ale. Alternatively, combine the ingredients, freeze in an ice cube tray, and then add a hot partner to the mix.

LORD OF THE MAI-TAIS

LORD OF THE FLIES (1954)
WILLIAM GOLDING

The plot that started a dozen TV franchises: Throw a group of disparate souls on an island after their airplane crashes, and, in a Clearasil-ready twist, make sure none of them are old enough to drive, let alone drink. If you went to a high school that favored broadened minds over banned books, you'll remember devouring this fable of order and disorder, schoolboys-turned-savages, and one very trippy pig's head. Recommended reading during your next flight to Hawaii, escape to the galley if things get bumpy and throw together this Polynesian nerve-calmer. It's fit to be served in a conch shell, but don't turn your back on the other passengers.

2 ounces cranberry juice
2 ounces orange juice
1½ ounces light rum
1 ounce coconut rum
1 teaspoon grenadine syrup (page 11)
Orange slice or pineapple wedge, for garnish (optional)

Shake the liquid ingredients with ice—odds are, it'll all turn out bloody red—and pour everything, including the ice, into a Collins glass. Get creative with the tropical garnishes: pineapples, oranges, eye of piglet...

HOW THE GARCIA GIRLS LOST THEIR APEROL SPRITZ

HOW THE GARCIA GIRLS LOST THEIR ACCENTS (1991)
JULIA ALVAREZ

Take a bunch of sisters, add not-so-healthy competition, parental repression, and some illicit romance, and you know you'll have a good story (looking at you, Jane Austen). The four Garcia girls, who grow up sheltered and pampered in the Dominican Republic, are in for a shock when politics get their papí in hot water and they all have to move to the Bronx. Although the girls' parents are old-fashioned, the sisters hit their bumpy stride, even as they lose sight of what's most important to them. There's poetry, prejudice, rebellion, humor, marriage, divorce, and complicated love of family in this wondrous, innovative, *quadruple* coming-of-age story.

3 ounces Aperol
3 ounces prosecco
1 ounce Puerto Rican rum (we like Bacardi)
1 ounce club soda
1 orange slice, for garnish

Fill a wine glass halfway with ice. Add Aperol, prosecco, rum, and club soda, then stir to combine. Garnish with a slice of orange. Add these ingredients forward or backward, and you'll have a spritz to savor on a hot summer city night. Multiply by four if you have sisters.

READ 'EM AND WEEP
BEAUTIFUL STORIES TO MAKE YOU UGLY-CRY

> How sad, a heart that
> does not know how to love, that
> does not know what it is to be
> drunk with love.
> —Omar Khayyam

There's something poetic about ugly-crying; if you haven't looked down at the page wondering if it's raining inside, only to realize tears are rolling down your cheeks faster than it took Heathcliffe and Kathy to fall in love, not to worry: We've got you covered. It takes real beauty and power to transport readers to a place of such intense emotion, and those works that do deserve their own special type of recognition. While we've concocted recipes to help soothe literary-induced heartaches, tissues are not included. Of course, if you're in a pinch, you can always turn to the page.

A COCKTAIL of TWO CITIES

A TALE OF TWO CITIES (1859)
CHARLES DICKENS

For readers of *All the Year Round*, a weekly journal that Charles Dickens published himself, it took over thirty issues to tell a tale set between Paris and London during the French Revolution. Though the cities are the real stars, there's a tragically romantic love story that plays out on their streets, starring a golden-haired beauty and the two men who are willing to die for her (talk about "the best of times"). Toast to sooty chivalry with our take on a famous drink that hails from the New York Bar in Paris: A Cocktail of Two Cities that requires nary a passport.

1½ ounces gin
¾ ounce Maraschino liqueur
½ ounce fresh lemon juice
¼ ounce Pastis
Champagne, to fill

Pour the gin, Maraschino liqueur, lemon juice, and Pastis into a shaker with ice, and shake well. Strain into a Champagne flute and fill to the top with Champagne. The result is *revolutionary*.

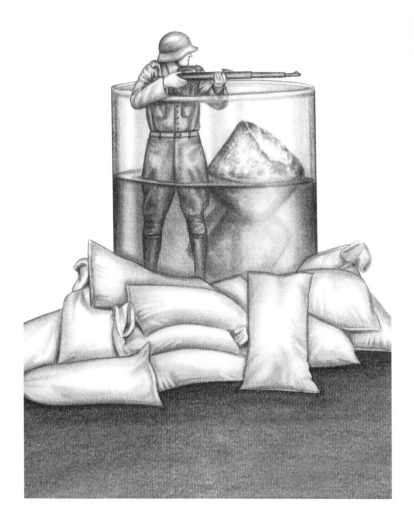

A FAREWELL TO AMARETTO

A FAREWELL TO ARMS (1929)
ERNEST HEMINGWAY

Widely lauded as Hemingway's most accomplished work, *A Farewell to Arms* firmly established his spare, just-the-facts prose. Little wonder: Before doing time as an ambulance driver in World War I, Hemingway was a junior reporter in Kansas City. Much of *Farewell* draws directly from Hemingway's own life abroad, from mortar shell injuries to angelic nurses. Nobody said war was easy, but just when you think the narrative is gonna land nice and quiet in Switzerland, Hemingway throws a friggin' dead *baby* into the mix. We salute Hemingway's complicated time in the Italian campaign with that country's own amaretto. Take this one like a tired toddler being put to bed: sour and fighting.

2 ounces amaretto
½ ounce fresh lemon juice
½ ounce orange juice
½ ounce Italian amaro (we like Averna)

Combine the amaretto, lemon juice, orange juice, and amaro in a shaker with ice. Shake well and strain over fresh ice in a rocks glass. For bonus points, serve in a nurse's uniform.

THE **SOUND** AND THE **SLURRY**

THE SOUND AND THE FURY (1929)
WILLIAM FAULKNER

A Southern family's tragic downfall, told from three distinct voices—
with a final, omniscient chapter—*The Sound and the Fury* became
popular only after one of Faulkner's later novels took off. With unre-
liable narrators who zigzag between suicidal impulses, confounding
stream-of-consciousness, *and an eye-crossing usage of italics*, this one may
have helped earn its author a Nobel, but it's no beach read. Set in a fic-
tional Mississippi town dealing with very factual post–Civil War growing
pains, *The Sound* inspires a cocktail that hangs on furiously to a traditional
Southern recipe—because some things are best left in the past.

    2 ounces dry muscadine wine
    1 ounce bourbon
    1 ounce orange juice
    1 ounce cranberry juice
    ½ ounce fresh lime juice
    1 (12-ounce) can root beer

Shake the wine, bourbon, and juices with ice and strain into a cocktail glass. Top with root beer. Alternatively, serve on the rocks—just
like your last family reunion.

TEQUILA MOCKINGBIRD

TO KILL A MOCKINGBIRD (1960)
HARPER LEE

Harper Lee's legendary novel is the oft-taught tale told by little Scout Finch, watching her Alabama town rally behind a lying drunk's lying daughter, who's up and accused an innocent Black man of taking advantage of her. Lucky for Scout—who watches from a courtroom balcony as her lawyer father defends the man—she's got levelheaded pals by her side, including Dill, who is famously modeled after Truman Capote. After a conclusion that leaves you both hopeful and haunted, toast to the continued evolution of our sometimes flawed justice system with a tequila shot that's guilty of packing a dill pickle punch.

1½ ounces reposado tequila
1 ounce dill pickle juice
1 dill pickle

Pour the tequila into a shot glass, add dill pickle juice, and slam that bad boy back before chasing with a big chomp of pickle on the side. No tears allowed here: If you can't stand the heat, get out of the South.

CALL ME BY YOUR NECTARINE

CALL ME BY YOUR NAME (2007)
ANDRÉ ACIMAN

Coming of age has never tasted so bittersweet. In André Aciman's steamy novel, a young Elio Perlman explores his sexuality with older, brainy Oliver, a summer guest assisting Elio's father with academic research. Elio quickly becomes enamored of Oliver, and their love affair blossoms and explodes against the backdrop of 1980s northern Italy— bella, *ciao!* Elio and Oliver, whose terms of endearment for each other are each other's names, struggle with their feelings, and ultimately have to reckon with a society not yet ready to welcome them with open arms. At its core, *Call Me by Your Name* is a lyrical ode to self-discovery and gives a whole new meaning to "peaches and cream." Take this potent cocktail slow and easy: After a few sips, you'll start calling it by *your* name.

2 ounces gin
3 ounces nectarine juice
1 ounce sweet vermouth
1 ounce cream liqueur
1 teaspoon grenadine (see page 11)

Combine the gin, nectarine juice, sweet vermouth, and cream liqueur in a shaker with ice. Shake well and strain into a martini glass. Spoon in grenadine and stir. Now that's *amore*.

THE **SONG** OF A **CHILE**

THE SONG OF ACHILLES (2017)
MADELINE MILLER

Who knew *The Iliad* was so hot? When Madeline Miller's mom read the Greek classic to young Maddy as a child, little did she suspect that her clever daughter would grow up to write possibly the most erotic Trojan War novel ever. Okay, *the* most erotic Trojan War novel ever. Most of us remember Achilles, the godlike soldier with the tricky heel. But who knew about Patroclus, his longtime companion and not-so-secret lover? Turns out it's hard to be domestic partners with a demigod (so touchy!). Make one mistake and the course of history is changed. *The Song of Achilles* has it all: sandals, cos-play, swordplay, Apollo, and a heart-shattering death scene that would make a bust of Homer weep.

3 raspberries, to muddle
1½ ounces mezcal
1½ ounces grapefruit juice
½ ounce chile liqueur (like Ancho Reyes)
Sparkling lime soda, to fill
3 raspberries, for garnish

Add 3 raspberries to a highball glass and lightly muddle until they burst. Pour in mezcal, grapefruit juice, and chile liqueur. Add ice and top with sparkling lime soda. Garnish with the remaining 3 raspberries and a sword cocktail pick. Then fold up your tent and call it a night.

UNLIKE WATER FOR CHOCOLATE

LIKE WATER FOR CHOCOLATE (1989)
LAURA ESQUIVEL

If there's a more fabulously sensual book than this one, we haven't read it (that includes you, *Fifty Shades*). In Laura Esquivel's voluptuous Mexican-set novel (with recipes!), Tita's fate is sealed the moment she is born: She must devote her entire life to caring for her mother (think: evil *Gilmore Girls*). But Tita is already desperately in love with ardent Pedro, and she doesn't know what to do with all that roiling emotion . . . except pour it into her cooking. This read is hot, so chill with some magical realism in the form of this heady Mexican-inspired cocktail.

1 tablespoon granulated sugar, for rimming
1 tablespoon cocoa powder, for rimming
2 ounces blanco tequila
1 ounce dark crème de cacao
1 ounce light cream
1 dash chocolate bitters
1 lime, cut into quarters
Chocolate shavings, for garnish

Mix the sugar and cocoa on a small, shallow plate. Rim a margarita glass with the sugar-cocoa mixture and set aside. In a blender, combine 1 cup of ice, tequila, crème de cacao, cream, and bitters. Add the juice from a quarter of the lime. Blend till smooth. Pour into the prepared glass, top with chocolate shavings, and don't be surprised if you suddenly burst into tears, song, or flames.

INTERPRETER OF MIDORIS

INTERPRETER OF MALADIES (1999)

JHUMPA LAHIRI

Heartwarming and heartbreaking, Jhumpa Lahiri's collection of nine short stories is a tapestry of cultures clashing, as she probes and explores the diversity of Indian culture, food, religion, love, and loss. Although the titular story "Interpreter of Maladies" is the best-known, there are many gems in this collection: "When Mr. Pirzada Came to Dine," about a Pakistani father's separation from his daughters in the midst of the India-Pakistan War; "The Treatment of Bibi Haldar," wherein a single woman's mysterious illness makes her a social outcast; and "This Blessed House," a story of newlyweds who keep finding Christian knickknacks. We dare you to read this book without stirring up an authentic vindaloo—or at least ordering in. Try this sweet and cooling cocktail alongside.

1½ ounces vodka
¾ ounce melon liqueur (we like Midori Melon)
½ ounce palm sugar syrup
¾ ounce fresh lemon juice
1 (12-ounce can) tonic water

Combine the vodka, melon liqueur, palm sugar syrup, and lemon juice in a shaker and fill with ice. Shake well and strain into a highball glass with fresh ice. Top with tonic water, and interpret as you will.

HOLD THE SAUCE

MOCKTAILS FOR THE SOBER SET

> It's a great advantage not to drink among hard drinking people.
>
> —F. Scott Fitzgerald

If you'd rather belly up to a good book with clear eyes, this chapter is for you. These non-alcoholic drinks are a tribute to the kinds of stories that are intoxicatingly beautiful—some are saucy, some are scrumdilly-umptious, and some are just plain supercalifragilisticexpialidocious (life hack: it's *so* much easier to say when you're not sauced). A mix of kid-lit essentials, this list has everything. So, put your (ruby red) slippers on, get cozy, and hit the sack early with these classics.

RIP VAN DRINKLE

"RIP VAN WINKLE" (1819)
WASHINGTON IRVING

A rare classic you can read in a single trip to the john, this short story packs a tall tale. In "Rip Van Winkle," one town's most lovable loner escapes his wife's overbearing personality by setting off on foot into the Catskills, a mountainous New York region that the then-bankrupt English author had never even visited—and this was pre-Google! Van Winkle happens upon a group of folks bowling in the woods (don't ask), enjoys a sip from their mysterious keg, and ends up taking a very satisfying nap. Like, twenty *years* satisfying. Appearing in the same volume as "The Legend of Sleepy Hollow" (remember the Headless Horseman?), "Rip" inspires a naptime-inducing drink that'll have you nodding off before even *entertaining* the thought of outdoor exercise.

Chamomile tea bag
Kiwi wheel, peeled
Honey, to taste

Brew one mug of tea and add the kiwi—known for its sleep-inducing properties—and as much honey as your wandering heart longs for. This drink is so soothing, you might want to set an alarm first.

THE **WONDERFUL**

BLIZZARD OF **OZ**

THE WONDERFUL WIZARD OF OZ (1900)
L. FRANK BAUM

If your knowledge of Dorothy (and her little dog, too) extends no further than the perennial classic film, you ought to take a look at the book that began it all—lest you miss the good stuff (killer bees; a crow-murdering Scarecrow) that didn't make it to the silver screen. Baum intended the novel as a one-time effort, but his publishers basically printed cash with his *Wonderful* words, and fourteen books in all appeared over twenty years. Follow your heart, freeze your brain, and have the courage to create a drink fit for a good witch: yellow as a brick road and swirly as a twister.

5 ounces pineapple juice
2 ounces coconut cream (like Coco Reál Cream
    of Coconut)
1 banana

Add the ingredients, plus a handful of ice, to a blender. Blend until smooth, and pour into a rocks or highball glass. Now, click your heels—or glasses—three times.

CHERRY POPPINS

MARY POPPINS (1934)

P. L. TRAVERS

An American favorite about a British nanny written by an Australian novelist. We all fell in love with Julie Andrews in the movie—and picked up a *terrible* Cockney accent from chimney-sweeping Dick Van Dyke—but this legend originated as a series of kids' books. Starring a stern but winking flying au pair, *Mary Poppins* understood tough love before daytime TV brought it into your mom's living room. We celebrate with a nod to Mary's home turf, Number Seventeen Cherry Tree Lane. This milkshake goes down so sweet, you won't even need a dash of sugar—let alone a spoonful.

1 scoop cherry frozen yogurt
4 ounces vanilla cream soda
5 maraschino cherries, plus 2 ounces of juice from jar
Splash of milk

Throw the ingredients into a blender with a handful of ice. Blend to desired consistency and serve in either a milkshake tin or a pint glass. For the love of Mary, make sure to garnish with an umbrella.

PAT THE TUMMY

PAT THE BUNNY (1940)
DOROTHY KUNHARDT

B ack when "interactive" meant reaching out and (novel concept, here) actually *touching* something, *Pat the Bunny* hopped onto the scene with wholesome, scratch-and-feel pages. Remember the sandpaper scruff on the dad? Or playing peek-a-boo with Paul (who was, frankly, too old to be playing peek-a-boo)? This quiet book made a loud dent, selling millions of copies and inspiring dolls, DVDs, and (don't pat *too* hard) even an app. We present a simple drink for long-gone times, back when a tummy ache would send you running to the nurse's office. Get back in the sandbox with one of these.

2 bags peppermint tea
3 slices fresh ginger*

Place the tea bags and ginger slices in a tall mug. Fill the mug with hot water and allow it to steep for 10 minutes. Let it cool, then strain over ice in a highball glass. Rest that weary belly—and then it's time to get bouncing again.

* Please note: Raw ginger should not be consumed by children under two.

FIREKEEPER'S TONIC WATER

FIREKEEPER'S DAUGHTER (2021)
ANGELINE BOULLEY

Let's raise a glass to Angeline Boulley: She thought up this story as a teenager and wrote it at age fifty-four. An instant young adult classic, *Firekeeper's Daughter* is a heart-thumping thriller about seventeen-year-old Daunis, who's caught up in an FBI sting of her Obijwe community. Things get complicated when she falls for Jamie, the mysterious new recruit on her brother's hockey team. Boulley keeps us all guessing about the plot, but not about her sure hand as a master storyteller in this page-turner of murder, drugs, herbs, and justice. For those who want to keep a sober head while reading, here's a refreshing tonic that will make you say *miigwech*. (You're welcome.)

1½ ounces tonic water
1½ ounces seltzer or club soda
½ ounce fresh lime juice
½ ounce simple syrup
3 dashes orange bitters
Fresh herbs (such as rosemary, thyme, or basil),
    to taste

Pour liquid ingredients over ice, stir in the bitters, and garnish with herbs. Mix with a hockey stick and skate away before the Feds come knocking.

THE **PHANTOM TOLLJUICE**

THE PHANTOM TOLLBOOTH (1961)
NORTON JUSTER

You'd think a fantasy this trippy woulda been written in the seventies. We all remember Milo, bored to tears with suburban life 'til a mystical tollbooth arrives in his bedroom. Milo hops into his toy car and drives on through, ending up in the Land of Doldrums (and you thought the Midwest was a yawn). He's not there long, because there are maps to ignore, folks to rescue, and clock-hawking hounds to befriend. Take your own trip back to summer camp, the boredom-busting destination where a mysterious "bug juice" has been served for eons. Reverse the clock with a color-changing cocktail that trades spirits for spirit.

MAKES ABOUT 8 DRINKS
1 packet powdered juice drink (like Kool-Aid,
     any flavor)
½ cup sugar
1 liter club soda
Lime, chopped into wedges, for garnish

Mix the Kool-Aid and sugar in a quart of water, then freeze in an ice cube tray. Empty the frozen cubes into cups, top with the club soda, and garnish with the lime wedges. Alternatively, go one cup at a time and save the rest of the cubes for later. Sometimes the best escapes are of the solo (or Solo cup) variety.

PEAR THE WILD THINGS ARE

WHERE THE WILD THINGS ARE (1963)
MAURICE SENDAK

Widely considered *the* children's book of all time, *Where the Wild Things Are* is the fantastical story of one boy's giant imagination, turning time-out in his bedroom into a trip to an island kingdom—complete with canoes, monsters, and one humbled temper. Believe it or not, this Caldecott-winning contemporary classic was banned widely when it first debuted—apparently parents and librarians didn't take a shine to such an angry child protagonist—but the kids didn't listen, sending Sendak to the top of their reading piles. Tame your own wild night out (not to mention that monster headache) with a hangover cure that'll stand the test of time.

4 ounces pear juice
2 ounces lemonade
2 ounces ginger ale

Combine the pear juice and lemonade over ice in a highball glass, then add the ginger ale. Now slip on your wolf PJs, draw the shades, and nurse that brain back to earth.

CHARLIE AND THE
CHOCOLATE FAKE-TINI

CHARLIE AND THE CHOCOLATE FACTORY (1964)
ROALD DAHL

The book that made us all long for our own golden ticket, *Charlie and the Chocolate Factory* was Roald Dahl's triumphant tribute to treats. Featuring an enigmatic chocolatier who has captured England's attention, *Charlie* finds five children, including our title character, winning a lucky pass inside the secret dessert lair, where the walls are lickable and the river is chocolate. Take a dip into a chocolate martini that loses the liquor, entirely suitable for curious kiddos—and their chaperones, too.

Cocoa powder, for cocktail rim (page 7)
1 Hershey's Kiss
1½ ounces chocolate syrup
1½ ounces light cream

Rim a chilled cocktail glass in cocoa powder. Drop a Hershey's Kiss on the bottom. Shake the remaining ingredients with ice and strain over the candy. Prepare for pure imagination.

PART

6

A LOAF OF BREAD AND THOU
BAR BITES FOR BOOK HOUNDS

> One cannot think well, love
> well, sleep well, if one has not
> dined well.
>
> —Virginia Woolf

Almost nothing pairs better than bar snacks and booze, except maybe the Mad Hatter and mercury poisoning. From olives to eggs to nuts, we've put together a spread that will leave you saying, "Please, sir, I want some more," in an accent no one can quite identify. So put away your shakers, jiggers, and strainers, pull out your mixing bowls, and get ready to call your relatives for cooking advice.

PRAWN QUIXOTE

DON QUIXOTE (1605)
MIGUEL DE CERVANTES

Quixotic, indeed: Fed up with the lack of chivalry in his day and age—and this was the 1600s!—the retired Alonso Quijano changes his name to Don Quixote, throws on a suit of armor, and sets out for adventure with a chubby sidekick and a skeletal horse. He meets sex workers, priests, and convicts, and if that sounds like a setup to a joke, you're right: *Don Quixote* is an elaborate romantic parody that, though written in two parts that were separated by a decade, is best consumed in one volume. Our classic shrimp cocktail gets a galloping-hot Spanish twist, with a result that's impossibly dreamy—and good fuel for your next quest.

MAKES 3 SERVINGS
10 to 15 fresh jumbo shrimp (about ½ pound), cooked
   and peeled
½ cup ketchup
2 tablespoons horseradish
1½ ounces fresh lemon juice
1 jalapeño pepper, seeded and diced
Salt and pepper, to taste
Hot sauce, to taste

Cook the shrimp (or thaw according to the package directions, if frozen). Combine the ingredients, except the shrimp, in a small bowl, then spoon the sauce into three stemless wine glasses—you know, the kind that wobble all over the place. Arrange the shrimp artfully along the glass rims, and your guests will be tilting at windmills.

ALICE'S ADVENTURES
in WONDER BREAD

ALICE'S ADVENTURES IN WONDERLAND (1865)
LEWIS CARROLL

Difficult to believe, but when Charles Dodgson's (aka Lewis Carroll's) *Alice* debuted, critics derided the bunny-chasing, hookah-puffing storyline as utter nonsense. Ah, *critics*: That was the point—and Carroll's enchanted world became inspiration for myriad films, musicals, and spin-offs. Bite into our mushroom treat, just like Carroll's daring darling might have. It might not make you taller, but it'll certainly leave you grinning like a Cheshire cat.

MAKES 1 SANDWICH
½ tablespoon olive oil
10 cremini mushrooms (about ¼ pound),
    roughly chopped
Garlic salt and pepper, to taste
2 slices white bread (like Wonder Bread)
½ cup shredded Swiss cheese

Heat the olive oil in a skillet. Add the 'shrooms and stir for 5 minutes. Sprinkle the garlic salt and pepper and remove from heat. On a plate or cutting board, top one bread slice with the cheese and add the warm mushrooms from the skillet. Scrape out any bits from the skillet and recoat with a little olive oil, returning to medium heat. Make a sandwich with your slices and cook each side for a few minutes until nice and toasty. And if anyone comes near your sandwich? Off with their heads!

OLIVES 'N' TWIST

OLIVER TWIST (1837–39)

CHARLES DICKENS

Charles Dickens knew his way around an empty belly: A one-time factory boy himself, Dickens was paid per *word* for his serialized novels, and *Oliver Twist* was an instant success with tabloid-hungry readers—even if critics called Dickens out for his shilling-seeking verbosity. Still, the adventures of a naive orphan who runs away, joins a gang of thieves, and ends up adopted by a wealthy family in the countryside remains good, if wordy, fun. Leave the gruel at the workhouse, because we're dressing up a college dorm appetizer in rich-kid clothes. Our lemon-twisted olives might compel your hungriest guests to beg for more, but this one's a cinch—and an Oliver-worthy steal.

MAKES 3 CUPS
3 cups mixed olives (all varieties)
2 teaspoons lemon zest
1 teaspoon olive oil
3 fresh rosemary sprigs
1 garlic clove, peeled and finely chopped
1 teaspoon dried red pepper flakes

Combine the ingredients in a jar or lidded container and give it a good shake—you've had enough practice after all these cocktails. For unexpected beggars at the door, serve in a bowl right away. Otherwise, keep this one in the fridge as a backup for lean times—provided those times arrive in the next couple of weeks.

FEAR OF FRYING

FEAR OF FLYING (1973)
ERICA JONG

Have your mate and eat him, too! Erica Jong's controversial, woman-liberating seventies novel follows a nearly-thirty poet on an overseas trip with her second husband. Our gal Isadora is not a happy traveler, so she decides to "fly," indulging her wildest sexual longings—with a different man than she arrived with. Groundbreaking at the time, *Flying* may go down as soapy and self-obsessed, but it takes off as a rule-breaking, hear-me-soar manifesto. Lose none of your favorite chip's zip with our guiltless snack, coaxing kitchen newbies with just three ingredients—since two is never satisfying enough for anyone.

MAKES 1 "POPCORN BOWL" OF KALE
1 bunch kale (about 4 cups, packed)
2 tablespoons olive oil
Coarse salt, to taste

This is a good, crunchy snack after a bad, crunchy breakup. Stop crying long enough to preheat the oven to 375°F. Wash and pat dry the kale, tearing it into bite-size pieces and discarding the stems. Toss the kale with oil and salt in a medium bowl, and then arrange on a cooking sheet so the leaves don't touch one another. Bake for 15 to 20 minutes (nursing a bottle of white wine while you're at it) and remove from the oven. Let cool for 5 minutes—and start making the next batch. You're gonna *blow* through these, so to speak.

THE DEVILED EGG
WEARS PRADA

THE DEVIL WEARS PRADA (2003)
LAUREN WEISBERGER

Hark! A movie version that actually ups the ante! Lauren Weisberger's roman à clef, allegedly paralleling her time as assistant to *Vogue* editor-in-*charge* Anna Wintour, was a dishy phenomenon, strutting to the top of the *New York Times* best-seller list for a nice long catwalk. Lit-turned-flick with megahit results, led by Meryl Streep's silver hair (and tongue) and Anne Hathaway in dumpy mode. Dress down this cocktail-party standby with healthy ingredients and Prada-bright paprika flakes. Remember: Every hall's a runway.

MAKES 12 SERVINGS
6 large eggs, hard boiled and peeled
1 (12-ounce) container of hummus
2 teaspoons fresh lemon juice
½ teaspoon white vinegar
Salt and pepper, to taste
Paprika, for garnish

Insult the eggs until they fall to pieces, or just cut them lengthwise and remove their yellow-bellied innards. Toss out half the yolks, mash the rest in a bowl with hummus, lemon juice, and vinegar, and spoon it all back into the empty holes. Now, take the most attention-grabbing lipstick-red paprika you can find and go to town embellishing: You never know when someone's taking a picture.

I KNOW THIS MUNCH IS TRUE

I KNOW THIS MUCH IS TRUE (1998)
WALLY LAMB

No literary conversation (or recipe book, for that matter!) would be complete without a nod to lifestyle brand Oprah Winfrey, who came undone for this author's earlier work. By the time *I Know This Much Is True* landed on her book club rotation, Wally Lamb was a bookselling bonanza. *True* follows the histrionic exploits of a pair of twins, one of whom pulls a Van Gogh on his own hand, chopping the poor thing off in a library. A meditation on the shadowed, sad, and very Sicilian history of one family, this novel is also a battle cry for mental health care in this country. You'll go wild for a candied mix that'll spice up any family gathering—whether it needs it or not.

MAKES 4 CUPS
4 tablespoons (½ stick) salted butter
4 cups mixed pecans and cashews
2 teaspoons garlic salt
1 teaspoon ground pepper
½ teaspoon cayenne pepper
Pinch of light brown sugar

Melt the butter in a pan over medium heat, about 3 minutes. Add the nuts and stir to coat. Add the spices and sugar, continuing to stir until totally dissolved, and then lower the heat and let cook for 8 to 10 minutes, turning the nuts throughout. Remove from heat, allow to cool off, and transfer to a serving bowl. These are so easy to enjoy, you could eat 'em single-handed.

THE **MUSTARD YELLOW HOUSE**

THE YELLOW HOUSE (2019)
SARAH M. BROOM

Most of us know New Orleans from Bourbon Street (daiquiri in a sippy cup, anyone?), but *The Yellow House* takes us to New Orleans East—specifically to a shotgun home known as "The Yellow House." A beautifully wrought tale of many generations and their connection to their family home, Sarah Broom's memoir is a poignant tribute to love, loss, and a New Orleans you won't find in a travel guide. Try this big, easy Cajun mustard for a taste of the real thing.

½ **cup mayonnaise**
2 **tablespoons honey**
2 **tablespoons grainy mustard**
1 **tablespoon Cajun seasoning**
⅛ **teaspoon cayenne**

Combine all ingredients, fire up some pigs in a blanket, cue some Preservation Hall Jazz Band, turn up the heat, and let the good times roll.

RED, WHITE, AND ROYAL BLEU

RED, WHITE & ROYAL BLUE (2019)
CASEY McQUISTON

Aromance that is royally unputdownable, *Red, White & Royal Blue* is the fabulously swoony story of Alex, the first son of the United States, and Henry, Prince of Wales and heir to the British throne. It's the classic prince meets prince story: Alex can't stand perfect Henry, and Henry may not be the stuffed shirt the tabloids think he is. After a spot of damage control to prevent a US-UK political fiasco, Alex and Henry are forced into a friendship, and, in a twist of fate, both un-friend-zone themselves into romance. With everyone against them, from Crown to commoner, will true love win out? Surprise your Prince Charming with homemade blue cheese dip, just the way they serve it at Buckingham Palace.

4 ounces blue cheese, crumbled
1 cup Greek yogurt
2 tablespoons fresh lemon juice
¼ teaspoon salt
Pepper, to taste

Combine all ingredients and serve it with pride.

BONUS!

DRINKING GAMES

....

DRINKING ALL BY YOUR LONESOME

Chug your ale each time Dickens introduces a new character in *Great Expectations*.

Pour a cold drink over your head every time you get too heated reading *Outlander*.

Take a sip of communion wine for every biblical sin you've committed. Start at Genesis.

Do a shot each time you look over your shoulder during *1984*. Two shots if you get up to close the curtains.

Slam a Red Bull every time you turn the page in *Wuthering Heights*. Just to stay awake, actually.

Never stop drinking during *The Nickel Boys*.

DRINKING WITH FRIENDS

Take turns trying to recite the infamous 11,282-word sentence from *Ulysses* in one breath. The person who stops first must drink most. (Responsibly!)

Get *x* copies of *The Shining* and *x* number of friends. In three rounds, race to find a specific word ("ax"; "hotel"; "scream").The last to find each has to take a shot of (red) rum.

Smuggle booze into a library. Play "Never have I ever" with the classics: "Never have I ever read *Beloved*," etc. All who have read the book in question must take a swig from the bottle. Scholars get smashed.

Divide into teams. Lay a giant old edition of *The Canterbury Tales* open on a table. Take turns bouncing quarters, attempting to land them on top of the book. The losing team—that which lands the fewest quarters—must present a drunk oral report on *The Canterbury Tales* by dawn.

Trade off reading any of Shakespeare's short sonnets aloud. After your turn, try to explain—in plain English—what the Bard was actually attempting to say. The person most obviously bullshitting must move to England and open a pub.

Each already-tipsy participant reads a passage from *Chinese Cinderella* aloud. Whoever cries hardest must be cut off from alcohol immediately. It is suggested that the group embrace and then gently rock them.

FORMULAS FOR
METRIC CONVERSIONS

....

Ounces to grams. . . . . multiply ounces by 28.35

Pounds to grams. . . . . multiply pounds by 453.5

Cups to liters . . . . multiply cups by 0.24

Fahrenheit to centigrade . . . . subtract 32 from Fahrenheit, multiply by
5, and divide by 9

METRIC EQUIVALENTS FOR VOLUME

US	METRIC	
⅛ tsp.	0.6 ml	
¼ tsp.	1.2 ml	
½ tsp.	2.5 ml	
¾ tsp.	3.7 ml	
1 tsp.	5 ml	
1½ tsp.	7.4 ml	
2 tsp.	10 ml	
1 Tbsp.	15 ml	
1½ Tbsp.	22 ml	
2 Tbsp. (⅛ cup)	30 ml	1 fl. oz
3 Tbsp.	45 ml	
¼ cup.	59 ml	2 fl. oz
⅓ cup	79 ml	
½ cup.	118 ml	4 fl. oz
⅔ cup	158 ml	
¾ cup.	178 ml	6 fl. oz
1 cup	237 ml	8 fl. oz
1¼ cups	300 ml	
1½ cups	355 ml	
1¾ cups	425 ml	
2 cups (1 pint)	500 ml	16 fl. oz
3 cups	725 ml	
4 cups (1 quart)	.95 liters	32 fl. oz
16 cups (1 gallon)	3.8 liters	128 fl. oz

OVEN TEMPERATURES

DEGREES FAHRENHEIT	DEGREES CENTIGRADE	BRITISH GAS MARKS
200°.	93°	—
250°.	120°	½
275°.	140°	1
300°.	150°	2
325°.	165°	3
350°.	175°	4
375°.	190°	5
400°.	200°	6
450°.	230°	8

METRIC EQUIVALENTS FOR WEIGHT

US	METRIC
1 oz	28 g
2 oz	57 g
3 oz	85 g
4 oz	113 g
5 oz	142 g
6 oz	170 g
7 oz	198 g
8 oz	227 g
16 oz (1 lb.)	454 g
2.2 lbs.	1 kg

METRIC EQUIVALENTS FOR BUTTER

US	METRIC
2 tsp.	10 g
1 Tbsp.	15 g
1½ Tbsp.	22.5 g
2 Tbsp. (1 oz)	27 g
3 Tbsp.	42 g
4 Tbsp.	56 g
4 oz. (1 stick)	110 g
8 oz. (2 sticks)	220 g

METRIC EQUIVALENTS FOR LENGTH

US	METRIC
¼ inch	.65 cm
½ inch	1.25 cm
1 inch	2.50 cm
2 inches	5.00 cm
3 inches	6.00 cm
4 inches	8.00 cm
5 inches	11.00 cm
6 inches	15.00 cm
7 inches	18.00 cm
8 inches	20.00 cm
9 inches	23.00 cm
12 inches	30.50 cm
15 inches	38.00 cm

Source: Sharon Tyler Herbst, *The Food Lover's Companion*,
    3rd ed. Hauppauge, NY: Barron's, 2001.

ACKNOWLEDGMENTS

Three cheers to Josh McDonnell and Lauren Mortimer on the gorgeous design and illustrations throughout.

A glass of rosé—even if we're in public—for Brenda Bowen, agent and all-around chief; research assistant Becky Goodman; and Cody Goldstein and Camille Parson at Muddling Memories for their knockout drink consultation.

And ninety-nine bottles of beer *off* the wall for Jordana Hawkins, editor and ally, and the entire team at Running Press. Thank you for getting this book and for *getting* this book.

INDEX

ABOUT THE AUTHOR

Tim Federle is the showrunner and executive producer of *High School Musical: the Musical: the Series*, which he created for Disney+. His novels include the *New York Times* Notable Book *Better Nate Than Ever* and its Lambda-winning sequel—which Lin-Manuel Miranda called "a wonderful evocation of what it's like to be a theater kid" (*New York Times*). A film adaptation of *Nate*, written and directed by Federle, was released in spring 2022. Federle co-wrote the Broadway musical adaptation of *Tuck Everlasting*, and won the Humanitas Prize for co-writing the Golden Globe and Academy Award–nominated Best Animated Feature *Ferdinand*, starring John Cena and Kate McKinnon. A former Broadway dancer, Federle was born in San Francisco, grew up in Pittsburgh, and now divides his time between Los Angeles and the internet.